MW00437871

# LEVERAGING STEREOTYPES
*to Your Advantage*

## TURNING STEREOTYPES INTO OPPORTUNITIES, FINDING BALANCE BETWEEN THE YIN AND THE YANG

# DIANNE LEE

# TESTIMONIALS

"In a raw and honest collection of real-life experiences, Dianne Lee shows us we shouldn't be limited by the color of our skin; in fact, we should capitalize on every opportunity to design a life that is limitless. Regardless of whether you are an Asian woman or are of a different ethnicity, you will see a part of yourself in this book. I appreciate the fearlessness that it took her to say yes and to share her struggles. This book will help you find your voice. Definitely a must read!" – *Helena Lin Jubany, FAIA, Managing Principal, NAC Architecture*

"If you've ever felt that society's stereotypes were holding you back from success and happiness, you'll find inspiration in Dianne Lee's heartfelt story as an Asian immigrant working in male dominated industries. Her perspective on navigating stereotypes to your advantage is empowering and insightful. Dianne intimately shares stories of encouragement, practical strategies and principles that will surely inspire and motivate you to live your best life now. The meaningful work she does today is a testament of my father's legacy." – *Patrick Conn, President, Charles Dunn Company*

"As an immigrant from India and a woman in a leadership role in the construction industry, I can confirm that what Dianne has gone through personally and professionally resonates with me. She has leaned on her core values and instincts to build on varied opportunities and diverse relationships as learning experiences. Her passion for life, her remarkable progress in the construction industry and her support for and promotion of women are part of her hallmark. Dianne's initiatives and tireless efforts are both admirable and welcome, especially with what we are witnessing today." – *Roshni Thomas, Director of Planning, Design and Construction, California State University, Dominguez Hills*

"Dianne Lee takes us on a vivid journey from her upbringing in multicultural Malaysia to the heights of influence in the construction industry. As our nation grapples with a rise in anti-Asian violence, this book serves as a timely reminder of the valuable contribution of new Americans and highlights the strategies one has used to succeed when the odds were stacked against her." – *Jay Chen, President of the Board of Trustees, Mount San Antonio Community College*

"Dianne shares her practical experience navigating the corporate jungle with poise, grace, and integrity. Her authenticity resonates deeply. Women confronting the paradoxical societal expectations of women and paving their own executive style will benefit from reading this book." – *Noel Hyun Minor, Real Estate CEO; Independent Attorney; Board Member of The Getty House Foundation and Central City Association*

"In this book, Dianne Lee expresses a level of vulnerability that few people are willing to reveal. By voicing the challenges minority women face in male dominated industries, Dianne illustrates the effectiveness of self-awareness and the benefits of holding steadfast to her core values. She courageously expresses her resistance to accepting cultural norms that continue to oppress minority women and ignore inequities and injustice." – *Rueben Smith, D.C.Sc., Vice Chancellor & Chief Facilities Executive, Facilities Planning & Development, Los Angeles Community College District*

"*Leveraging Stereotypes* is a powerful book about sharing your authentic truth. By leveraging the journey and path forward, she shares how she has garnered credibility and respect by sharing her knowledge and by giving respect. By being self-motivated, she's created a platform for personal and professional success. Dianne is paying it forward for all women regardless of ethnicity. A must read, especially if you are a woman in a male dominated industry!" – *Julie Owen, Deputy Executive Officer, Program Management, Los Angeles County Metropolitan Transportation Authority*

"The discussion around being more self-aware is as important as ever and a great reminder that each of us brings something unique and valuable to every discussion. We must support and empower each other to create that equitable society for all." – *Ryan Patel, Global Business Executive; Board Director at Drucker School of Management; TV News Contributor*

"Dianne's unique story as an Asian immigrant is powerful and profound and reflects her ability to master every challenge that comes her way. In *Leveraging Stereotypes*, she shares effective strategies and techniques to discover your platform and to advance your business network. What she shares is a proven method on how to build authentic relationships. This book reminds us of the important values from our upbringing and brings us back to the basics of approaching others with kindness and respect while discovering our best self." – *Alexander Kim, Deputy Director to Former California Governor Arnold Schwarzenegger*

"In reading Dianne's story, I was reminded of my own challenging path towards authentic leadership and finding my own voice in a world where I was often the only female in the room. Dianne's journey of self-awareness is an inspiration for anyone who is striving to live and lead authentically. When we are truly able to leverage our strengths and to acknowledge the power of our differences, we all become better. Her commitment to lifting others up through her own experiences and life story is inspiring. I am grateful to have her as a colleague and I look forward to supporting her continued success." – *Wendy Cohen, President, Kitchell CEM*

"Dianne Lee harnesses the environment and the people around her as a source of strength and commitment to realizing her true purpose. She is a professional who continues to find ways to improve herself, her company and the industry! It has been a pleasure to watch her grow and accomplish amazing things not just for herself, but for everyone else around her and I am truly humbled and honored to have been her mentor." – *Guy Mehula, Former President, Parsons International; Former Chief Facilities Executive, Los Angeles Unified School District; Retired United States Navy Captain.*

# DEDICATION

This book is a tribute to my parents and all the men and women who have served as mentors and supporters of my journey and have encouraged my efforts, my successes, and my overall well-being. To my late brother who was killed at 46 in Malaysia in a senseless and reckless freak accident. May he continue to enjoy the music he used to play for us and may he continue to sing with the angels. And to the future supporters who will be coming into my life as advocates, inspirational leaders, and disruptors; I look forward to meeting you.

This book is dedicated to the small but brave percentage of women who are and continue to be in the architecture/engineering and construction industry, and to the amazing bosses who recognize our value and have been bold enough to encourage and support our ideas and contributions. Thank you for giving us the freedom to spread our wings and the opportunity to have a voice. To the millions of women in very male dominated industries who have given us — women — a reason to continue believing and fighting the good fight, I say thank you for your support and for giving us your shoulders to stand on.

To my Asian sisters: regardless of your origin, I am inviting you to create your own platform so you can have a voice. Let's build on the momentum of advocating for each other and support the movement of leveraging stereotypes to our advantage.

My experiences and relationships in this book are authentic, are based on real-life experiences, and have been a real blessing towards finding my voice, my courage, and ultimately my platform.

# TABLE OF CONTENTS

# INTRODUCTION

## Definition of Stereotype

### A widely held but fixed and oversimplified image or idea of a particular type of person or thing.[1]

In social psychology, a stereotype is any thought widely adopted about specific types of individuals or certain ways of behaving intended to represent the entire group of those individuals or behaviors as a whole. These thoughts or beliefs may or may not accurately reflect reality.[2]

Everyone at some point in their life has probably faced some level and some form of stereotype. You don't have to be Asian or a minority or a person of color to be stereotyped.

This book reveals my experience with stereotypes as an Asian woman in a male dominated industry. The stereotypes have come in varying shapes, sizes, forms, and levels. Stereotypes are a very complex, over-generalized belief, sometimes offensive and hurtful, but channeled in the right way and under the right circumstances and environment, they can be beneficial. This is my story of how being

---

1   See the *Oxford English Dictionary*.
2   Park, Bernadette, and Charles M. Judd. "Rethinking the Link Between Categorization and Prejudice Within the Social Cognition Perspective." *Personality and Social Psychology Review* 9, no. 2 (May 1, 2005): 108-30. https://doi.org/https://doi.org/10.1207%2Fs15327957pspr0902_2.

stereotyped has not only given me an advantage but has allowed me to earn the respect of my peers and has led me to my dream job and life.

## Definition of Yin Yang

**The ancient symbol of harmony reminds us that life is a balancing act and most fulfilling when we learn to embrace dualities: the ups and downs, good times and bad, joys and challenges.[3]**

Similar to the concept of leveraging failure to learn from those mistakes and come out on top, you can also leverage stereotypes to elevate your growth, presence, and ability to meet and exceed expectations for positive outcomes.

Some of the more common and typical Asian stereotypes are that Asian women are naturally smart, submissive, great at math, and all the same – they look the same, sound the same, speak the same language, and only marry the same kind, etc. (you get the picture). They are willing to do almost anything that is asked of them, have very strict parents (aka "tiger moms"), are bad behind the wheel, and are uniformly high-achieving individuals.

I am not an expert in stereotypes, but I have been able to successfully navigate some of these preconceived notions in my personal and professional life that have contributed to my growth and success. My hope is that through my stories, you will find your own unique way of dealing with stereotypes to come out stronger, better, and smarter.

**"Twenty Ways You Can Tell You Have Asian Parents. Number one on the list: Your parents never, ever call you 'just to say hello.'" — Kevin Kwan, Singaporean-American Novelist, Writer of Satirical Novel *Crazy Rich Asians***

---

3    Original source unknown.

CHAPTER #1

# EMBRACING THE YIN AND THE YANG

In Ancient Chinese philosophy, yin and yang is the concept of dualism, describing how seemingly opposite or contrary forces may actually be complementary, interconnected, and interdependent in the natural world, and how they may give rise to each other as they interrelate to one another.

Based on this philosophy and belief, I want to inspire and encourage you to embrace who you are and what you have; the person you have become and the individual you want to become. With a global pandemic affecting all of us and as someone with an outward facing and highly sociable position in my career, despite so many months of self-isolation, I am determined to not let this pandemic get the best of me. Instead, I have resolved to create a positive outcome for myself. In the midst of so much uncertainty, I stay inspired by others who give themselves so willingly by sharing a vision that benefits the greater community.

As an example, I was energized by Andrew M. Yang, most recently known as the Asian Democratic candidate in 2020. Andrew is an

American tech entrepreneur and philanthropist who was originally a corporate lawyer. Andrew chose to rise to the challenge by throwing his name in the hat in the recent primaries. He used his voice and platform to bring more awareness and to highlight key issues central to his campaign. In 2019, he released his book titled *The War on Normal People*, which focused on the challenges of job displacement, automation, and universal basic income (UBI). Initially considered a longshot candidate, he gained significant support in early 2019 and gave millions of Asian Americans a sense of belonging, hope, something to get behind, and more importantly, something to get excited about. What Andrew started was a movement on behalf of Asian Americans, one that I admired and respected.

Despite dropping out as a presidential nominee, Andrew continues to leverage the movement and platform he has established. In January 2021, he announced his run for the Mayor of the City of New York.

Another visible and highly accomplished individual is 2016 Pulitzer Prize winner Viet Thanh Nguyen. Viet shares the story of his parents' entry into America and how their grocery store (Saigon Moi meaning my Saigon) served Vietnamese families in San Jose, California beginning in 1978, and was a symbol of pride, self-determination, and defiance. He shares their story as refugees to America — tales of heroism and hope — and continues to speak about their sacrifices, contributions to the community, and their pursuit of the American dream. Honoring his parents' legacy, today Viet is a professor at the University of Southern California and an op-ed columnist for *The New York Times*. He utilizes his voice and platform to bring attention to immigration, refugees, politics, culture, and Southeast Asian issues. In 2020 Viet Thanh Nguyen joined the Pulitzer Prize Board as its first Asian-American and Vietnamese-American member.

Both Andrew Yang and Viet Thanh Nguyen embraced the yin and the yang, have exceeded expectations, and have shattered glass ceilings. By using their voices and their platforms, they continue to educate and give back to the greater community. At a time when Asians in America are being marginalized for their association with the COVID-19 pandemic, these two individuals continue to rise to the occasion by speaking of the contributions minorities have made in support of the growth of the American economy.

In 2020 and into 2021, we witnessed how damaging derogatory and stereotypical comments can be, especially towards certain ethnic groups. We also saw how much hate and violence can come from these comments, and so we must take this opportunity to learn from what we witnessed and experienced and turn it into positive outcomes. In this book you will read about the frequency of micro aggressions with which I was faced when starting out in my career and how often being an Asian woman comes with specific expectations and judgements, but you will also learn about how this has shaped my perspective and how I have been able to apply these stereotypes to support my growth.

My story starts as a young girl born and raised in a rural town in a Muslim country, Malaysia. I am Chinese by ethnicity, Catholic by religion, Malaysian by nationality (since Malaysia is my birth country), and American by citizenship. I am the American story.

I spent the first 17 years of my life growing up in a beautiful tropical Muslim country. Malaysia is a country located in Southeast Asia, south of Thailand and north of Singapore. If you have never been to Malaysia, I would highly recommend adding the country to your bucket list. If you are an architecture enthusiast, then Malaysia will definitely not disappoint. Its fascinating mix of elements with Islamic design, colonial influences, and Asian traditions offers a blend of modern and post-modern mixed architecture. The colonial buildings that still exist today were built towards the end of the 19th and early 20th centuries. And if you are a foodie, I promise you, after spending a few days in Malaysia you will leave with a completely different take on Asian cuisine. The tantalizing flavors, aromatic spices, and rich concoctions will forever change how you enjoy every meal.

Although it will take you over 19 hours to get there from California, it is a beautifully exotic tropical country with a lot of natural beauty. Its diverse population is warm, genuine, and welcoming, and the combination of different cultures offers a perfect blend of Malay, Chinese, and Indian influences. Malaysia is a country that has a unique ability to leave you coming back for more.

Malaysia is a multiracial country with many different ethnic groups. The demographic composition in the country is: 50.1% of the population are Malay, 22.6% are Chinese, 11.8% are indigenous groups other than the Malays, and approximately 7% are Indians who migrated from India. This multicultural context makes Malaysia quite a rich society, with diverse religions, foods, cultures, and customs.

Indigenous to the country, the Malays are the largest ethnic group. As was mentioned above, the Chinese are the second largest ethnic group in the country, and this is the category under which I fall. Helping to unite this diversity is the national language, a standardized form of Malay, officially called Bahasa Malaysia. It is spoken by most Malaysians and growing up under the country's government school system I learned all subjects from age six to 17 in this language. That included math, science, history, geography, and biology, to name a few.

I paint this picture because as a kid growing up in a multicultural country, we were never exposed to any form of racism or stereotype. We never talked about it and our parents never had a reason to bring it up. Growing up in the '70s and '80s especially, Malaysia was a great representation of harmony within diversity. We proved that people of different religions, creeds, castes, languages, cultures, lifestyles, fashion senses, faith in God, rituals of worship, etc. could harmoniously live together.

We not only respected each other as friends and embraced each other's differences and culture, we also celebrated and participated heavily in each other's customs. As a Chinese girl I was invited to partake in my friends' religious holidays and celebrations and in Malaysia we acknowledged and celebrated all religious holidays. We had mosques, churches of all denominations, and temples, both Buddhist and Hindu. We embraced everyone's differences and we never questioned their beliefs, culture, or religion. The only question we asked each other as young kids was, "See you same time tomorrow?" Our playdates involved friends from different ethnicities.

I was born and raised in a very small rural town named Klang. Today Klang is a 45-minute drive northeast to the capital city of Kuala Lumpur. As a young girl growing up in the '70s there was only a one-lane freeway (parts of which were a dirt road) to get to the city and only a one-lane freeway to get back. It wasn't a pleasant journey; in fact, there were times when it was flat-out miserable. Let's just say, I hated being in the back seat! It used to take up to 90 minutes to get to Kuala Lumpur for some decent shopping and popular dining experiences. And if it was in the middle of the monsoon season, it could take over two hours to get there and another two hours to get back.

The monsoon season would bring torrential rains, which caused major flooding. In the '70s Malaysia was still a third world country and it didn't have the proper infrastructure in place to mitigate the heavy tropical downpours and the growing traffic demands. So back then we didn't quite have the major freeways and overpasses/

toll roads to enjoy the ride to the city. For entertainment and some excitement, however, heading into the capital was the only option and many Malaysians would spend the weekends meeting up with friends and relatives there. Today, Kuala Lumpur is a bustling and vibrant international capital city with a diverse population of over eight million residents and Malaysia is a country with over 32 million people.

Klang was a simple town with basic amenities. I remember we got our first bowling alley in the center of town only in the '80s. The town of Klang is known for its port, so it served as the main gateway by sea to Malaysia. In 2012, it was the 11th busiest container port in the world. When I was growing up the town had a population of about 100,000 residents and because of its rurality, I had a very humble and typical upbringing by Malaysian standards.

I grew up in a middle-class Chinese family in a modest three-bedroom house surrounded by other Chinese, Indian, and Malay families in an extremely diverse neighborhood. The front yard was filled with orchids, roses, and bougainvillea. A papaya and two mango trees filled the backyard – one of the many advantages of living in a tropical country. My mom continues to obsess over her garden today. The neighborhood was safe, and my parents never had to worry about me getting into trouble.

As a young Chinese girl, you always knew your boundaries, and you always knew that how you acted in public was a direct reflection on your parents and the family's last name, which carried a lot of weight and pressure. With the Lee last name came responsibility, accountability, and pride. For the most part, my friends and I were always extremely polite, well behaved, respectful, and helpful. That sort of behavior is considered the gold standard by most families. That is the culture with which most Chinese Malaysian kids are raised. Any misstep, bad grades, rudeness, or disrespect would be a direct representation of your parents and their lack of control over their children. So as children, my friends and I always strived to please our parents, to make them proud, and to ensure that only positive comments were made. In that way, we could make our parents proud of our existence.

I attended an all-girls school from the age of seven to 17. For 10 consecutive years, I wore a perfectly pressed dark blue and white school uniform, with perfectly laced white shoes and a perfect ponytail. Those were the rules and standards imposed. It was a public school overseen by the Malaysian government, but it had British and Catholic influences because Malaysia was a country governed by the British before independence in 1957. The British influence carried over to our school system, which means we operated under the structure of having a primary and secondary education system.

Most of my friends were smarter than I was, painful to admit as an adult but that's the truth. They were mostly book smart; we were all too young then to figure out if we were street smart yet. I do remember though growing up with friends who always scored straight A's. It didn't matter what subject it was, how little they studied, or if they never studied at all – they still scored perfect A's. They were gifted, had great memorization skills, or were amazing test takers. I on the other hand didn't quite have the combination of all those skills.

Even at the early age of seven my classmates had already lived up to the Asian stereotype of being smart and hard-working; they were straight A students and were impeccably behaved – a typical expectation in most Asian cultures. I used to envy them. As for me, I had a hard time sitting still and paying attention in class. I figured out I enjoyed school because I enjoyed being with my friends, learning about them, and seeing what made them different and fun. To me that was far more interesting than understanding science, history, or (worse!) math. I despised every math test I had to take. I used to have nightmares before every math exam. I was the kid who preferred climbing every tree to see what the view was like from up high and thoroughly enjoyed riding my bicycle through the many neighborhoods. I enjoyed the outdoors and always sought adventure. To me, the outdoors was the best classroom any kid could ask for.

Some of you may know that there is a stereotype of people of Chinese or Asian descent being naturally great at math. You may be laughing, but that's an actual stereotype. Well, I am living proof that that is not true. My anxiety the night before a math exam was real and no amount of extra tuition lessons after regular school could make a difference. I just wasn't wired that way. However, in hindsight, I am grateful for this sort of expectation, because once I realized how it could work in my favor, I saw that I could capitalize on such expectations for my personal success. Unfortunately for me, I wish I had figured this out much earlier, for example in high school. I would have approached the math exams differently and possibly received better grades.

One of the many things I do appreciate about growing up Chinese is that you always knew what would upset your parents and you just stayed away from those things. Similarly, you always knew what would make them happy and proud and so you were always aware of how to meet and exceed their expectations.

This structure and fairly clear and strict upbringing proved beneficial for me. I unconsciously enjoyed knowing that my parents had high expectations of me, and I lived to make them proud. There was nothing more fulfilling than hearing your parents refer to you as a "good girl" to their friends and relatives. It was like a "mission accomplished" moment every time they uttered those words.

I am the youngest of three kids. My older sister Daphne is independent, athletic, and enterprising, while my older brother, Alan, the firstborn, loved music and lived for it. Alan, as the oldest child, was meant to carry the family last name forward. Unfortunately, on April 26th, 2010, that legacy was abruptly taken away from all of us. Alan was 46 when he was killed in a freak accident.

I remember the sacrifices my parents made to give us what we needed and some of those sacrifices included not having any family vacations. In fact, I can't remember more than one family vacation from the time I was five until I was 17. But when you grow up in an environment not talking about family vacations, you just don't know any different; you don't know how you are missing out and I honestly never felt deprived.

My best childhood memories are of my days competing at swim meets and tennis tournaments. I lived for those days! I was born to compete and enjoyed all aspects of the training that would lead to the actual competition; even more so, I enjoyed winning. Both Mom and Dad were competitive. Dad was an avid tennis player and Mom was great at badminton. They both loved to sing and dance. It's what drew them to each other; they were the perfect singing duo. Singing karaoke is their favorite thing to do. How Asian! Even my parents lived up to that Asian stereotype. I do believe I inherited their competitive nature (but sadly not their singing voices) and being in sports further ignited my competitiveness despite my petite 5'1" physique. I am forever indebted to my parents for ensuring that even with what little we had as a family, I was signed up for those extracurricular activities that ignited the competitiveness in me. It probably explains why I enjoy being in business development today; it truly is a team sport that involves collaboration, communication, teamwork, endurance, strategy, persistence, and determination.

Speaking of determination, I remember both parents working a lot. Mom was a trailblazer in her own right. She started an adhesive tape packaging business in Malaysia in the early '80s at a time when women were not encouraged to be working, much less running a company. She had an entrepreneurial spirit and not being successful was not an option. I see now in my 40's where I am so much like her. She refused to give up even when she was surrounded by naysayers, when people would steal from her and try to cheat her out of her own business. She was relentless when it came to providing the best customer service to her clients and worked day and night to exceed their expectations. She understood clearly what having her own business meant and the sacrifices that would come along with it while raising three kids. She was always ready to support her clients and always responded when they needed her. I used to watch her in awe of her work ethic while meeting and juggling the demands of a very competitive and flourishing industry.

Contributing to her success was the industrial boom in Malaysia in the late '80s. She started her business when the country was at the height of its industrial boom; factories were popping up everywhere and large U.S., U.K., and Asian based firms were opening up assembly facilities all over the country. Mom had client accounts servicing multiple large factories for goods that were assembled in Malaysia and exported to the rest of the world. And like a typical Chinese business owner, she worked six days a week and sometimes seven.

Despite her newfound success, we stayed humble – we never ate at fancy restaurants; we maintained our simple lifestyle and had very basic meals of rice, fish, chicken, mixed vegetables, and porridge (congee) and were only allowed to look forward to having KFC (yes, fried chicken) for dinner once a month. Back in those days in Malaysia, the American influence had not yet dominated the Asian market, so getting a bucket of KFC was always such a treat for the family.

I also remember getting only one gift at Christmas each year and was always so grateful to have the luxury of receiving that one gift. As a young girl growing up in a very modest household, I was never allowed or encouraged to ask for anything extravagant, so no brand-name products, no trendy outfits, no watches, nothing from an American catalog, and nothing we saw on TV. Plus, it was considered disrespectful and rude to ask for or even expect a gift. We were often reminded to be grateful to have a roof over our heads, to have food on the table, and for the privilege of attending public school.

Perhaps my favorite possession, however, was my red and black BMX bicycle, which allowed me to roam the neighborhoods with my friends. Like clockwork, every evening after regular school, after extra tuition classes, and after all the schoolwork had been completed, a group of us would meet up and for hours we would go from one neighborhood to another, enjoying our freedom while staying within the boundaries of being well behaved kids. That bicycle gave me some of the best memories I could ever have asked for.

I will say that one of the best things about growing up in Malaysia was the diverse culture and the safe environment that existed. My parents never had to worry about me going missing or being taken advantage of. In general, the Malaysian culture was a very supportive and safe environment; everyone knew everyone else and your neighbors were always looking out for you. The only thing my parents ever had to worry about was me falling off a tree or falling off my bicycle, which did happen more than I'd like to admit. Or worse, falling off in grades, which also happened more than I'd like to admit.

Besides that, I could leave the house and as long as I was home just before my parents got home from work, it was pretty much a stress-free family environment.

Which brings me to this: while I was born ethnically Chinese and raised in Malaysia, I've been living in America since I was 17. I arrived as a foreign student in 1992 and was fortunate to have been given the opportunity to attend Indiana State University.

I had my fair share of positive and negative experiences as a foreign Asian student in the Midwest. I am thankful that 90% of my experiences were positive ones but it's always those one or two negative experiences that you remember for life – the way someone looks at you and worse, the way someone says something to you that is totally unwarranted. Despite that, I've not let these negative experiences dictate the quality of my education and my life as a foreign student. I am reminded that my parents spent their entire life savings to give me the education I needed to be successful and I am eternally grateful for their foresight and commitment to giving me a life better than what they had. I stayed focused on why I was given the opportunity to come to America and thoroughly enjoyed the college experience. There was a lot to love and appreciate about being in the Midwest, having met some of the nicest and most genuine people from Terre Haute, Indiana.

**"Often, the truly great and valuable lessons we learn in life are grasped through pain. That's why they call them "growing pains." It's all about yin and yang. And that's not something you order off column A at your local Chinese restaurant." — Fran Drescher, American Actress ("The Nanny"), Comedian**

# CHAPTER 2

# WELCOME TO AMERICA, LAND OF THE FREE, HOME OF THE BRAVE

As a foreign student in America and in particular the Midwest, I noticed that most of my friends saw Asians as one race and often assumed we were all from one big country or from one big region. The Asians, however, never felt or acted that way. The Korean students stuck with other Korean students and the students from China stayed within their kind as well. As Malaysians we were also somewhat cliquish, but we did welcome and integrate with the Indonesian and Singaporean students, perhaps because we spoke similar languages.

I learned upon arriving in America that there were varying levels of stereotypes. As an example, we don't all speak one universal language. Not all Asians speak Chinese or Mandarin, to be specific. In this sense, we are not like the Mexicans, Spaniards, and many South Americans, for whom Spanish is the universal language (albeit there are different variations). Wherever Spanish is spoken, it will generally be understood by other Spanish speakers, even when they speak different dialects. When I conducted my research for this book as to how many Asian languages there are in the world, even Google had a hard time providing an educated and accurate response. With over 4.5 billion people across the continent, there is an estimated number of over 2,300 languages, and those are the ones that we actually know of.

My point is all Asians are not from one colossal country or region. We may share some similarities, which I realize can be extremely deceiving and confusing, but we are all extremely different. The reason the Koreans, Japanese, Filipinos, Indians, Indonesians, Singaporeans, Malaysians, Thais, Vietnamese, and many other Asian ethnicities are so distinct is that we all have our own languages, cultures, customs, and beliefs. This clearly adds to the varying degrees and levels of stereotypes that Asians face.

My ability to transition, embrace, and adapt to my new lifestyle and community in the small college town of Terre Haute, Indiana took bravery, naiveness, and a sense of adventure. I will also be the first to admit that learning what a windchill was and what "minus degree weather" could do to your body also required some form of bravery. Let's just say it wasn't one of the most enjoyable experiences, especially for a girl from a tropical country where temperatures averaged between 80 and 95 degrees Fahrenheit all year round.

It also didn't take me long to figure out as a freshman that my professors and peers judged me for how I looked, how I sounded, and believe it or not, how well I performed as a student. Those relationships and perceptions could make or break your entire college experience. There was the stereotype that as long as I was Asian (any kind of Asian), I was naturally smart, didn't have to spend a whole lot of time studying, and (again) was great in math. Little did they know that I actually had to work really hard in every class and for every grade above a C. What did come naturally to me were two subjects: English and geography. I used to win primary school spelling bees in Malaysia and always excelled in geography. I thoroughly enjoyed learning about the different cultures, which explains my curiosity and love for international travel today.

My command of the English language started at the age of six. Mom used to make me read the *New Straits Times* (the Malaysian version of *The Wall Street Journal*) out loud. Even though she knew I didn't understand what I was reading, she would correct my diction and then ask me if I knew what a particular word meant. And then we would pull out the dictionary and discuss the meaning and how we could best use it in a sentence. At that time, the dictionary was the largest and heaviest book on the shelf. Thankfully, Mom kept the dictionary in the lowest level of the bookcase so that I could get to it. I could barely lift it with my little hands.

The only board game I remember playing at the age of six was Scrabble. Mom loved Scrabble and she always asked me to bring out the board after dinner. I owe my reading, writing, and spelling skills to her. When I decided to attend college, it was no surprise that I would choose a major in broadcast television news with a minor in journalism. I wanted to be the next Connie Chung, a famous Chinese newscaster in America in the '80s.

Majoring in television news had many benefits, allowing me to have the career I have today in business development. It really sharpened my writing, listening, and communication skills, which are critical to the success of any business developer.

Terre Haute, Indiana had some severe winters and campus parking was always an issue, so we spent a lot of time walking from our cars to class on one side of the campus and then walking back again from one building to another to make the next class. By the time I put on the three or four layers of clothes and jackets to keep me warm, I was barely recognizable behind the scarf.

I do remember two stereotypical comments that were made while I was walking to class with a group of predominantly American friends. The first one happened during my freshman year. One of them said to me, "Hey, Dianne, do you know that girl across the street?" I looked across the street as the snowflakes drifted across my red cheeks and then looked at my friend, and I asked, "Why would I know her?" He said, "Because she's Asian, so don't you all just know each other?" I realized he was being silly and so I laughed along. Ha! Ha! And brushed it off as I dusted away the snowflakes hitting my face.

Then in my senior year, I started hanging out with a new group of friends from a journalism class and one of them asked me where I was from. I said very generically, "I'm from a country called Malaysia in Southeast Asia," not expecting her to know where Malaysia was located. Without hesitation, she asked, "Does that happen to be a country we own? You know, like Hawaii." Yes, she said Hawaii. She didn't even identify Hawaii as one of the United States of America. I wasn't sure how to react to that, but I also knew to not let such comments offend me and affect my relationships with my peers. I politely smiled and said, "No, it's not owned by America, but it does have some similarities to Hawaii."

I embraced everyone's differences even if that meant that they were unaware of other cultures, geographic origins, histories, and sensitivities. I didn't expect my American friends to understand my origin and culture. After all, this is a big world and there's lots to learn, explore, and understand. It was that approach and mindset that got me through many other stereotypical comments and awkward situations in college. Regardless of the stereotypes I continued to maintain all of my relationships, I enjoyed everything about the college experience, embracing the yin and the yang and where I had the opportunity to educate my friends about my story and my country of origin, I did.

Unfortunately, for some foreign Asian students, they don't get the opportunity to educate their peers and to share their story. I witnessed Asian students who were sidelined for having an accent, for being too smart, for asking too many questions, and for being different.

In my sophomore year, I had a Japanese friend named Yuko; she was probably one of the brightest students in my study group. She was an introvert who always kept to herself. I always knew where to find her – on the second floor of the Cunningham Memorial Library.

Yuko was shy and never raised her hand to ask a question in class. She didn't want to be stared at and didn't want others to judge her. She felt more comfortable asking one of us (Asian students) and many times she would just figure things out on her own.

Yuko spent a lot of time at the library. She was always seated in a corner with her head down reading a book she knew nothing about. One evening, I went over to check in on her (I was social even back then as a college student) and I asked her, "What are you reading?" She went on to respond, "A book off shelf." Then I noticed a huge dictionary next to the book she was reading, and it occurred to me that as she was reading, she was looking up words she hadn't seen before and didn't understand. I remembered that that was the same thing my mom had me do when I was six years old. Staring at the dictionary on the table brought back memories of my time in the house in Klang.

Yuko would write down words that were unfamiliar to her on a notepad with Japanese characters next to each word. She was reading each sentence and taking down words she didn't understand from the book and then looking up their definitions and uses, and adding Japanese words next to each word, so she wouldn't forget the meaning. It seemed like such an arduous and painstaking process and I wasn't sure at that moment if I should start crying because I felt bad for her, or if I should give her a hug to congratulate her for her determination to want to excel as a foreign student in America. I decided instead to let her continue studying so as to not break up the rhythm and focus she had established that evening. Watching her in the corner studying under those fluorescent lamps in the library, night after night, made me ask myself this: What are you willing to do to be successful and how will you overcome your challenges?

Just like Yuko, I too had an accent, but I have never met anyone who struggled with her accent and the English language so much and yet continued to excel by consistently averaging a 3.5 GPA semester after semester. It was really impressive. How did Yuko do it? English was clearly not her first language, but she loved studying — obviously much more than I did — and she was great at taking exams; she would memorize the vocabulary and would piece together her responses. This showed me that in her own unique way, she found a means of expressing herself in a foreign language, understood the theory and concept behind a topic, and then aced every test. I watched her in amazement and admiration of her determination and creativity to rise to exceed everyone's expectations, especially those of her professors and her parents. She was just an incredible student and chose to not let her shortcomings determine her future. She embraced the American college education system and experience and in four years graduated and returned home to Japan. Better. Stronger. Smarter.

Yuko took a yin (her challenges with the English language) and pushed forward by converting it into a yang. Her ability to overcome her language barriers left a lasting impression on me. I never got to thank her, but I realized much later how watching her study in the library impacted the last two years of my college experience.

The answer to the questions I had asked myself didn't appear immediately, they lingered for months; they came and went.

In the blink of an eye, summer was gone, and fall had arrived, and it was time to pull out the thick winter coats, the scarfs, and the gloves again. Sigh. I went about my semester not even giving the questions of what I was willing to do to be successful and how I would overcome my challenges a second thought. Almost a full year had gone by before I realized it.

I was in the middle of my junior year and the course work was now more focused on radio and television writing, broadcasting, interviewing, and communication skills. My eagerness to learn more about being a great news reporter just like my idol Connie Chung gave me a level of excitement and exhilaration I can't explain. I enjoyed learning how to craft and tell a compelling story, how to make something relatable, and how to provide the facts necessary to back up and complement a news story.

Then one day, I noticed that I was consistently getting B's for every course work in broadcast journalism. I knew my content, I did a ton of research to back up my stories, and I wrote fairly well as a foreign student from Malaysia. I always followed instructions, took extra classes to gain extra credit, and still was not obtaining the grades I had expected. I couldn't figure out what it was that I was doing wrong or not doing sufficiently. So, I went to one of my journalism professors.

Professor Duncan was pretty stern and strict when it came to class instruction; he was always clear about what was expected of us. He hardly smiled and I wouldn't refer to him as extremely approachable; he definitely made me nervous. He was, however, a phenomenal professor, succinct and fair, a no-nonsense kind of man, and I was so grateful to be in his class. He was definitely one of my favorite professors. After class one afternoon, before throwing on my scarf, I mustered up the courage to ask him for a meeting. I was thrilled when I made it onto his calendar.

The day finally came, and I was anxious and nervous. I didn't waste any time and asked what I could do better to get to an A grade. He told me that he saw how hard I was working but that one thing would always hold me back if I wanted to make this my career. I sat in anticipation. Was it the way I looked? Was it my writing skills? Was I just not good enough? Did I not have what it takes to be a reporter? Then, he shared with me something I had not expected.

He told me that my accent didn't do me any favors; in fact, it was an impediment. He said that while my presentation skills had potential, my accent didn't allow me to be taken seriously. I just didn't sound intelligible and universal enough. So regardless of how well I wrote my news stories and reports, the accent didn't add to my credibility; in fact, it took away from it. He suggested that some of his students had sought out accent coaches like an acting coach who could help teach different accents and thought that would be a way for me to learn how to fix my pronunciation of certain words along with adjusting my delivery and intonation. He said this issue wasn't exclusive to foreign students, stating that even Americans who are born and raised in Indiana were also encouraged to take speech lessons to work on their delivery.

I am so glad I took the time to meet with Professor Duncan. I really appreciated his constructive criticism and started to seek out how I could sound more comprehensible and credible. Even I knew at a young age that a reporter needed to look and sound the part and lacking credibility would be detrimental to a reporter's opportunity of landing a job at a television station. I took his suggestion seriously and started researching how I would go about getting the coaching needed so I could make the proper adjustments.

In my research, I learned that a speech coach was not going to be cheap and the best ones were located in Indianapolis, an hour's drive from the college town of Terre Haute. Furthermore, getting appointments during the week while attending class on campus was going to be impossible. My parents had already sacrificed so much to get me to America and enrolled in college; there was no way I was going to ask them for more money to support my speech class. I remembered Yuko's creativity and her tenacity, and I decided that if I couldn't afford a speech coach to help me sound more like a credible reporter, then I was going to somehow do it myself.

I remembered how when I was six my mom would make me read out loud and she would correct my pronunciation of big words. I thought if I watched enough American news and practiced on my own to sound more like them, then perhaps that was a method that could work. So, for hours I would watch and study Dan Rather, Katie Couric, Ann Curry, and Peter Jennings. They were my personal speech coaches. I didn't have to drive anywhere to see them and I certainly wouldn't have to pay for their services. Then I would pick up the local newspaper and would read out loud for hours. I would continue reading out loud until I was convinced that I had started to sound more and more like them. I spent around six months watching and listening to them, and over time, I noticed that I started to sound more professional, more mature, and definitely more credible.

My parents would visit my sister and me in Indiana once a year and on one of their visits, Mom made a comment. She noticed that I started to sound — in her words — "more American." She was quite surprised. I reminded her that I was majoring in broadcast journalism and that I had to "fix" or alter how I spoke not only to get the grades I wanted, but to sound more audible to a greater group of people.

My practice sessions in front of the television turned into how I eventually speak and sound today. I also learned that the better I spoke, the more respect I garnered and surprisingly enough, the better I presented myself. Finally, in my senior year, I started getting the A's I had been waiting for. Professor Duncan congratulated me for the improvement in how I delivered my news reports and presentations in class. He acknowledged that my hard work had paid off, stating that he saw a dramatic difference in just a few months and knew a lot of people who had struggled with their accents for years.

Prior to my conversation with Professor Duncan, I had a very distinct Malaysian accent, which was a blend of Chinese dialects, Malay, and hints of the British English influence. I spoke the Hokkien dialect with my aunties and uncles; Cantonese to my grandmother; Malay to my friends at school, and English to Mom and Dad. Like many others from a similar upbringing and environment, I sometimes used a mix of two to three languages all in one sentence, so much so that in Malaysia, many Malaysians spoke a combination of English and Malay and we would refer to that as "Manglish."

What I learned from this experience was that I was able to modify how I speak without any professional help. I accomplished this task out of sheer determination and commitment to myself because I wanted to be taken seriously as a journalist in whatever country I wanted to be reporting out of. I wasn't going to accept defeat because of my accent. I got creative and did what I had to do. Once I realized I had the ability and power to make changes in my life so rapidly, especially with an accent that I had grown up with for 20 years of my life, I began to discover my confidence and couldn't wait to contribute to society in a more meaningful way. I decided to speak up more when it mattered and to use my voice to enhance the relationships I had established.

I am grateful for my time as a foreign student at Indiana State University, having met some of the nicest, most genuine and welcoming individuals and families. My exposure to the Midwest has given me a deeper understanding and appreciation for America. I have fond memories of the kindness of the people and many beautiful seasons and will forever cherish the time I was given while I was there.

Once I graduated from college, I pursued a career in the television news industry and continued to experience additional stereotypes to which I felt I had to live up. Initially, the experience was confusing and stressful but the more I figured out how to leverage those stereotypes and take advantage of what was expected of me, the more focused I became on my trajectory. As a news reporter, you are expected to gather the facts and make sense of everything in minutes, write your story, capture your sound-bites and then look amazing in minutes. And because I am Asian, I was expected to excel in all those categories in minutes… joking! But you get the picture: it was indeed a very fast-paced industry, and everything always seemed like a mad rush.

I'll be the first to admit that overcoming stereotypes almost seems like an impossibility but with the right approach, mindset, and determination, the stereotypes can propel you by accelerating your learning curve and eventually placing you in a more advantageous and fruitful position. I know they did for me. All those expectations made me a better presenter, a better writer, and definitely a better communicator. I also picked up the skill of deciphering information and relationships very quickly.

After eight years of being in the broadcast television industry as a news reporter, I was fortunate to make a really interesting career change. I decided to go into the real estate and construction industry. It was almost serendipitous. As if being in the television news industry hadn't been challenging enough, I threw myself into an industry about which I knew absolutely nothing. Add to that the complexities of my outward-facing role in a professional environment as an Asian woman and an immigrant in a primarily male dominated industry – the construction industry.

This is why this book is more about leveraging stereotypes and not necessarily overcoming them. What I am about to share with you are some real-life stories about my professional and personal growth from the construction side of the business. The book chronicles some of the best lessons learned from my career and some of the challenges I've had to face and turn into positive growth opportunities: everything from mean girls to disrespectful colleagues; from unwanted sexual advances to acknowledging some of the best male mentors any girl could ask for.

My hope is that the following chapters of this book will inspire you to want to do more for yourself, with the goal of advancing your career. This book will give you many different perspectives and at the same time, I hope the messages will resonate with your personal and professional life. What I want for you is a better, kinder, and brighter future, with the aspiration that it will somehow move you to identify your core values, your worth, and your contribution in service of others around you.

This book hopes to serve as a reminder that despite life's many challenges and our personal shortcomings, the sun will continue to rise and set, and it is up to each of us to continue the journey by being brave; by lifting ourselves and each other up. I've spent the last 15 years as an Asian immigrant in a very male dominated industry and I want you to know that you are not alone and that being under- or overestimated is an opportunity to perform and over deliver. What a great concept!

Now despite the many stereotypes, let's find the yin and the yang together after all….

**"The only person you should try to be better than is the person you were yesterday." — Anonymous**

# CHAPTER 3

# IF YOU CAN READ, YOU CAN COOK. HOW WELL YOU COOK IS UP TO YOU

## — Mom

I've been tremendously blessed and have had the opportunity to travel across five continents and over 30 countries. I am sharing this not to brag about the many travel destinations or how many immigration stamps I've collected over the years in my passport, but to paint a picture of how these adventures and the people I have met along the way have shaped and influenced who I am today. My love for international adventures has been a blessing in multiple ways.

In most of my travels, the one consistent message that has come up over the last 10 years is from the individuals I have had the pleasure of meeting over these exotic international trips. Ironically, most of them have encouraged me to tell my story. They have found my humble and simple upbringing both inspiring and interesting and are usually eager to learn more about who I am and how I got to where I am today. Additionally, they've found my success to be somewhat intriguing. Usually after spending a few hours together sipping Turkish coffee in Istanbul or sipping matcha tea in Tokyo, Japan, sharing a long road trip through the Annapurna mountains in Nepal, or while practicing yoga at a retreat in the Maldives, they've often suggested that I write a book about being born in a small town in Southeast Asia and making it in America. It's a bit of a rags to riches story that many have found unbelievable and inspiring.

After consistent random requests from perfect strangers while exploring and touring foreign countries, in the last three years or so, I started to take the formulation of this book seriously. I began collecting my thoughts and making mental notes. What you are about to embark on is a collection of circumstances and experiences, negative and positive life lessons, and messages about how we can take advantage of the stereotypes we face on a daily basis and turn those into positive outcomes to advance our personal and professional goals.

You may know that sometimes you hear something so many times that it seems like the Universe is trying to tell you something. Well, that is exactly how I would describe the birth of this book.

While I was in the process of writing, someone asked me why publish this book now? My response was that, in the same way the pandemic has triggered many moments of reflection and gratitude for a lot of people, I felt a sense of calling and obligation to share my struggles and to speak to how stereotypes can affect us, but more importantly, how they can influence a brighter and more fulfilling future.

Current events around the world have highlighted that everyone's lives matter, regardless of age, color, ethnicity, gender, status, origin, and background. And the combination of the COVID-19 pandemic and racism issues have taken center stage. We have seen how severely impacted our society has been and have been told we should expect an increase in mental health problems. Did you know that nearly one in six Californians experiences some form of mental illness?[4] To make matters worse, one out of every 24 will be seriously affected by any variation of stress. It will become that much more difficult for them to function in daily life. So much so that if left untreated, the illnesses will not only impact their quality of life but could also impact the individual's ability to survive.

Having spent the last 15 years as a resident in LA County, which has the largest homeless population in the world, I have noticed that mental health is a frequent topic of conversation in the City of Angels. The Los Angeles County Department of Mental Health (LACDMH) is the largest county mental health department in the United States. LA County's Public Works Department has an entire construction capital improvement program dedicated to constructing temporary treatment and housing facilities for mental health patients called Restorative Care Villages. This is a societal issue that affects all of us, and when the negative effects of racism and stereotypes persist, coupled with the effects of self-isolation because of the pandemic, the likelihood of an increase in mental health cases is undeniable. The human cost is too great to ignore. We must acknowledge and show through our actions now, how we can help and support each other better. We also need to figure out how, as individuals, we can better manage and navigate these harmful perceptions.

In 2020, the frequency of anti-racist sentiments highlighted in news broadcasts particularly resonated with me. Stereotypes play a central role in this discussion and I felt compelled to represent Asians by sharing something positive that stems from something so negative. Personally, I couldn't think of a better time than now to share how our differences are what makes each of us unique and great

---

4   California Health Care Foundation, "Mental Health in California: For Too Many, Care Not There," March 2018, https://www.chcf.org/wp-content/uploads/2018/03/MentalHealthCalifornia2018. pdf.

contributors to society. I am excited to reveal how the stereotypes I've had to face have brought me considerable fulfillment and have allowed me to accomplish and attain my dream job and life.

Life is indeed full of surprises, and I will never forget this conversation with my mom. It happened in 2007. I had been approached by a real estate mogul, one of the nicest and most successful men in the commercial and residential real estate business in Los Angeles, Walter Conn, Senior. Of course, when I first met him, I had no idea who he was, but he encouraged me to join his firm Charles Dunn Real Estate. The company provided real estate brokerage and property management services. And Walter Sr. — that was how most of us addressed him — was the chairman of the firm.

Walter Sr. saw something in me that I didn't even know I had. He saw my potential and took the time to get to know me, my upbringing, and my story. I later learned that Walter was notorious for recruiting hundreds of individuals who would all end up working with him, ensuring success not only for the firm, but also for the employee whom he took the time to mentor and support. Walter Sr.'s approach was simple: hire the right people with the right attitude and gratitude, and then give them the right platform on which to be successful. And that's what he ended up doing for me.

I remember the day I was offered the position and called my mom for her advice. I was extremely apprehensive and second-guessed the opportunity to work for Walter Sr. as I knew nothing about the real estate industry or about business development. I waited for the right time to call her as Malaysia is 16 hours ahead of Los Angeles, California, and I didn't want to wake her up in the middle of the night. I wouldn't be living up to the Chinese daughter expectation if I were to be that inconsiderate and disrespectful.

Once I got mom on the phone, I began to tell her about how I met Walter Sr. and how he had offered me a position at his firm. Here's how my mom responded: "What have you got to lose? You know how to read, don't you?" There was silence from my side of the telephone. She followed up with, "If you can read, you can cook, but how well you cook is up to you. So, when do you start?" I submissively responded, "Well, right away," and asked her again if she was sure I should take the job. She reiterated that how well I did at the position was going to be entirely up to me. She reassured me that she had done her part as a parent by giving me all the tools to make all the right decisions to be successful and that I would eventually figure things out. And with that, I said yes to Walter Sr. and started almost immediately. I have never looked back.

Walter Sr. was always more concerned with the well-being of his business associates, employees, and anyone else he encountered than his own. His door was always open to lend an ear, give advice, and help anyone needing him, and he did all of that with so much grace and wit. I can honestly say, if it wasn't for Walter Sr.'s ability to see my potential, I wouldn't be where I am today and I certainly wouldn't have the career I have today. It's funny how life works. I also realized that I was hired because of my ethnicity and my story. He understood the culture and environment in which I was raised and knew what he was getting: a hardworking, respectful, humble, committed, and dedicated employee who was eager to prove herself in America. I was the epitome of the stereotype of an immigrant and he saw value in that. I, in turn, lived up to what he expected of me.

Walter Sr. took me under his wing and truly served as my mentor. I shadowed him on a daily basis, I took notes, and I paid attention. I saw how he approached his business dealings and how he would successfully close deals. I saw how respectfully and eloquently he spoke to people. I saw how he juggled his schedule, taking unexpected quick turnaround trips to Asia, getting on a flight to Tokyo to view a piece of property for purchase and jumping right back on the next available flight to Los Angeles in two days, and he did all this in his 70's. I saw how he always made his family and employees a priority while juggling and prioritizing business interests.

Walter Sr. loved touring potential real estate sites available for purchase and he enjoyed visiting existing sites under his portfolio. He was always excited about life and people. On a daily basis he was stoic, professional, and even funny. He was shrewd in business, was a master negotiator, and treated everyone fairly with kindness and grace. Walter Sr.'s genuine care for others gave him access to a network of people who admired and were loyal to him. He showed me how in business the relationships you cultivate and nurture are the lifeline of longevity and an established reputation.

Walter Sr. left a legacy of generosity with his time and words, and his ability to see the value in people brought out the best in everyone around him. To show you what Walter Sr. was really like, years after I had left Charles Dunn Real Estate and taken on new positions, when Walter Sr. heard about my brother's passing, he took the time to send me this letter.

May 3, 2010

Ms. Dianne Lee

Dear Dianne:

I was deeply grieved to learn of the tragic demise of your brother. My heartfelt condolences to you and your family. May God give you the strength and the courage to bear this irreparable loss. Your brother will be in my prayers.

With Sympathy,

Walter Conn

My point is, if channeled in the right way, great things will reveal themselves. Walter Sr. based his decision to hire me on a stereotype with which he was familiar, and I rose to meet that stereotype. It was a win-win for him and for me. I am eternally indebted to him and his family for giving me the opportunity and the platform to grow into the person I am today. Unfortunately for so many of us whom he inspired, Walter Sr. passed way too early from cancer. In 2014 over a thousand people came together to show our respect and our gratitude. I miss our conversations over lunch at the historic Jonathan Club in Downtown Los Angeles and especially miss his great sense of humor.

Little did I know, unbeknownst to me, that accepting this position with Charles Dunn Real Estate and saying yes to Walter Sr. in 2007 would go on to expand my industry network far beyond what I would have ever imagined. I had no idea that working for him would open up so many doors and segue into a career in which I thrive today.

"Embrace what you don't know, especially in the beginning, because what you don't know can become your greatest asset." — Sara Blakely, Founder of Spanx, an American intimate apparel company. In 2012, Blakely landed on the cover of *Forbes* magazine for being the youngest self-made female billionaire in the world.

# Chapter #4

# Hope Takes You Through the Fire, Faith Leaps You Over It

## — Jim Carrey, Comedian

I have always admired stand-up comedians. It's hard enough to be a public speaker, but to be on stage and attempt to make people laugh at your jokes is a whole other ball game.

It's estimated that as much as 75% of the population struggles with a fear of public speaking to a certain degree. Some individuals may feel a slight nervousness at the very thought of public speaking, while others experience full-on panic and fear, and for that I am truly inspired by Jim Carrey. Many of us know him as *Ace Ventura, Pet Detective*; some of us know him better from *Dumb and Dumber*. Jim Carrey is known for his ridiculously energetic, funny, slapstick performances. When I learned that he had a hard time making friends as a young child and suffered from dyslexia, I was fascinated by how he became so successful in show business. One would simply assume that he was just always great with people, but that was not the case.

He was socially awkward growing up and his learning disorder added to his insecurity and lack of confidence.

In an interview that documents his journey, he shares that his unconventional approach is what allows him to be so funny today. He shared with the reporter, "I might not make it through the front door, like everyone else. But I'll make it through the basement window. I'll make it through the back door. I'll find a way to parachute in on the roof and climb down into a window."[5] It is this sort of determination and tenacity that spoke to me. Jim realized that being funny and entertaining was a way to make friends and so he kept working on being funnier and funnier each day. His creativity and desire to succeed paid off.

Today, Jim Carrey has a net worth of $180 million and his unique ability to keep us laughing and entertained is priceless.

I would say he figured out how to leverage the yin and turn it into a yang. Like Jim Carrey, most of us are faced with all sorts of challenges – some we are born with and some are just perceptions others have imposed on who we are as individuals. Either way, there is always an opportunity to turn something negative like a stereotype into a positive.

To further validate this concept, I remember watching *Happy Days* while growing up in Malaysia. In the '80s in Malaysia, we only had three channels to enjoy: two government television stations and one private station. I grew up at a time when DVDs and DVRs didn't exist, so KFC and *Happy Days* were all the American influence we got.

I am grateful that *Happy Days* was one of the sitcoms that aired on Malaysian television. Henry Winkler, who was best known as Fonzie in the sitcom, also had to overcome several personal challenges. At a

---

5    "Jim Carrey's 'Nonsensical Belief' in Himself and the Universe," *CBS News* (CBS Interactive, July 5, 2020), https://www.cbsnews.com/news/jim-carreys-nonsensical-belief-in-himself-and-the-universe/.

young age he was also diagnosed with dyslexia and referred to himself as stupid. He thought he was too dumb to ever be successful. In his mid-70's and after a highly successful career in show business, he is today the author of 30 books. In an interview with James Corden of *The Late Late Show*, Mr. Winkler said, "You don't know what you're capable of until you try it, so don't let anything stop you from being successful."

Once I left Charles Dunn Real Estate and joined an architectural firm as a business developer, I continued to experience additional stereotypes related to being an Asian woman in the architecture, engineering, and construction industry. I found that a few of the principals consistently challenged me – some more than others. One in particular just had it out for me.

At first, I didn't quite understand why; I was naïve. I always felt that if we were all batting on the same team, we should be supportive of each other and not trying to undermine each other. I almost immediately became a target at every team meeting (thankfully, our meetings only took place once a week), and after six months of working with the individual who had it in for me, it just got unbearable.

I later learned from another colleague who was also Asian — Korean to be specific — who happened to report to her, that this principal felt threatened by me, my work ethic, my client network, and my keen ability to over deliver, even though we had completely different positions and both of our goals involved identifying new opportunities with new clients for the benefit of the entire firm. I observed this individual consistently leading by imposing fear on others, especially individuals of a certain status and without the big titles, and she always kept everyone at bay. When she needed support, she never hesitated to ask for it and when she didn't, she had the power to make you feel as if you never existed. I never understood

why she never respected me as a colleague and why she would attempt to make me feel like nothing I said mattered, even though I
would bring new client relationships that would increase the firm's
revenue and expand our collective portfolio.

My intuition led me to ask myself this question: would she have
treated me differently if I had sounded or looked more like her?
Would she have been more welcoming and collaborative and less
disrespectful? My gut response is yes.

Being stereotyped can impact your emotional and physical being
and I relied on my instincts to help me define the relationship. You
don't necessarily have to hear for yourself any derogatory remarks;
sometimes being stereotyped is a feeling and it is so personal that
only you alone can determine the nature of the relationship.

So patiently I waited. For months I hoped that she would just
start being nicer to me. We didn't have to be best friends, but it would
have been great to just have mutual respect for each other. I waited
for the opportunity to collaborate and the opportunity to strategize
with her, most of all to win work together. Once again, I was being
naïve. I thought how great it would be to have two dynamic women
join forces as a team; we would have been a force to be reckoned
with. But that opportunity turned into wishful thinking and never
materialized. She went on her way and I did mine. We were both
independently successful and stayed in our own lanes. To me, it
was such a missed opportunity to accomplish even greater things on
behalf of the firm we both represented.

I never complained about the way she made me feel, nor did I
share it with any of my supervisors because I wanted to handle it
like a professional and not allow personal attacks to hinder my position or the relationships and reputation I had worked so hard to
build within and outside of the workplace. I stayed focused on what

my team expected of me and always over delivered where I could. That was my healthy distraction: I poured every ounce of energy into my job to deflect how she treated me. My successes helped me stay sharp; I knew I was doing something right when we were being presented with more opportunities from new clients, so I focused all my energy on staying the course instead of her stereotypical judgements and actions directed towards me.

In hindsight, she was really doing me a favor. Her judgement of me and her insecurities about having me as a colleague encouraged me to become a better, more diligent business developer for the firm. Thanks to the way she would dismiss and disrespect me, I started preparing more intentionally before the weekly leadership team meeting. I started to do more research so I could respond to every question she would ask in an attempt to try to embarrass me in front of the other principals, and when the team would expect two or three new leads, I would present three times the number that was expected of me. Her "meanness" made me stronger and smarter and strengthened my resolve.

I really owe her a debt of gratitude for undermining and for underestimating my potential. The chip on her shoulder and ego imposed on me made me work even harder and inspired me to learn my craft even more. Her unbecoming treatment ignited my passion and drive to be the best in the industry. To further amplify my position, I made sure to have my best outfit on for our weekly meetings. This also helped spark my interest in fashion, which continues today – something I am also grateful for.

This negative (yin) experience turned positive (yang) truly catapulted my career. In the two and a half years at the architecture firm I can confidently say I quadrupled the number of client relationships I had and expanded my industry network again far beyond what I could have ever imagined.

Here I was, a 20-something-year-old with no family ties in California – no aunties or uncles with high level connections. I had just moved to Los Angeles a couple of years earlier and was literally making my mark in a predominantly white and male dominated industry. I found myself networking with some of the most powerful, politically connected, and influential individuals in the Los Angeles business community, some of whom I still share a great meal with today.

This environment of progression, unlimited possibilities, and the excitement of uncovering a platform for acquiring new relationships was where I realized I had transitioned from having a job to having a career.

And my gratitude and love for America continued to grow.

Then, in 2010, when America was still in the middle of the world financial crisis of 2008, what was famously referred to as the modern-day Great Recession, I took a leap of faith. I had the opportunity to become an expatriate. An expatriate, also known as an expat, is a person who lives outside his or her own country while working abroad. By this time, I had become a proud U.S. citizen.

One of my mentors, Guy Mehula (someone I truly respect and admire), was asked to take on the position of President of Parsons in the Middle East region. He would be based out of Abu Dhabi in the United Arab Emirates (UAE) and would be responsible for 3,000 employees across five countries (UAE, Turkey, Kingdom of Saudi Arabia, Oman, and Qatar). He was tasked with growing and further enhancing key client relationships. I was beyond elated when he asked me to join him there to help advance and support the growth of the company. I jumped at the opportunity and didn't hesitate in saying yes to the new and exciting position. I had by that time traveled and visited several continents but had never explored the Middle East region. In just under two weeks, I sold everything I owned including my brand new gray metallic Honda Accord and was on a 17-hour flight to the United Arab Emirates. This is the country made famous by Sarah Jessica Parker and Kim Cattrall of *Sex and the City 2*.

The overall experience of living, working, and learning all about the Middle East region and culture was enlightening, worthwhile, and exhilarating. People often ask me how I "survived," and I gladly share that it was one of the best and most memorable experiences of my life and that I am so grateful to have had the opportunity to acquire the knowledge of conducting business internationally and being an expat. I grew tremendously professionally and personally and learned so much about the booming construction industry in the Middle East. I owe a huge part of my success as a business developer today to having had this incredible and unique experience.

The Middle East region hosts expats from all over the world. In the United Arab Emirates, expats make up 88% of the total population. Combined with the local people, known as the Emiratis, it made for a very diverse and absolutely unique environment in every aspect. With its cuisine, lifestyle, fashion, and many adventures (I got certified as a diver in Abu Dhabi), it offered varying perspectives and an immersive culture.

Abu Dhabi is the capital of the UAE. When showing up to work it was like working for the United Nations. That's the simplest way for me to describe it. You could hear over a dozen different languages and accents spoken on any given day. Of course, the universal language is English and that's how we all communicated with each other. Being Chinese and raised in Malaysia, my ability to speak multiple languages definitely helped me comprehend the different accents and cultural differences better.

The workload in the region was consistently demanding and stressful because we were catering to government clients who could pretty much afford whatever they wanted and were willing to spend billions of dollars on contracts, and naturally that came with high expectations and unrealistic timelines. To counter the stress, most expats would jump at every opportunity to travel to one of the many neighboring countries. I was no different. Because the UAE is centrally located in the Middle East and is an easy destination to get to and from many neighboring countries, I had the opportunity to visit the Great Sphinx of Giza in Egypt; ride a camel in Doha, Qatar; visit the ruins of Petra in Jordan; tour the Blue Mosque in Istanbul, Turkey, and visit many other interesting and beautiful countries (Seychelles, Sri Lanka, Oman, Nepal, Maldives, and Hong Kong, to name a few). This was definitely one of the many positives of my life as an expat.

While living and working there for over two years, I discovered how progressive, open, and receptive everyone was to each other. Because of that, I instantly made many new friends, some of whom I continue to stay in touch with. I have even traveled to new destinations with some of them since returning to America.

While I thoroughly enjoyed my time working in the Middle East, there was unfortunately one individual — a female — who was not thrilled about my arrival. Although it was a much less negative experience than my time at the architecture firm, it was no less annoying and unnecessary. This individual developed negative perceptions of me and felt threatened as soon as I stepped off the plane.

Daniella (not her real name) was a few years younger than me. She was smart, pretty, and ambitious and had been with the company for over five years by the time I arrived in the region.

Despite my attempts to be cordial, respectful, and careful so as to not upset or intimidate her, her insecurities got the best of our working relationship. My job as an expat was to support the team and elevate our efforts in any way I saw possible; to identify and streamline opportunities for efficiencies; to elevate the quality and content of our proposals by ensuring compliance with company standards, and to represent the firm at all conferences, client events, and meetings as necessary. We were to work side by side to jointly create a better marketing and business development process and a greater, more comprehensive approach to the market and the region. She had the opportunity to learn from me what the "mothership" was doing and I had the opportunity to learn from her how the Parsons Middle East region team had become so successful.

But from day one, I was treated as an unwelcome threat. Other Asian team members warned me about her, which I appreciated. I never liked walking unprepared into the lion's den. Apparently, her dislike of others was felt by a few other Asian team members as well, so there was clearly a pattern to her behavior. Her lack of collaboration, offensive and inappropriate comments (mostly done behind my back) pushed me into a space I never thought I could occupy in the workplace. She approached me as a person by relying on a stereotype and was clearly intimidated by me and everything I had the potential of doing.

There was nothing I could do about her lack of engagement and willingness to respect what I was tasked to do for the betterment of the firm, and there was nothing I could do about her negative perception of me. Despite all my attempts to get to know her, she continued trying to compete with me instead of collaborating with me. We eventually learned how to work with each other, but we never became trusted partners, and it saddens me that that was the best we could do.

The negative aspect of this experience, however, did remind me that I can't control how others respond or react, what I am able to control is how I respond and react to others and I chose to respond with dignity, respect, and patience. I am, after all, the only one accountable for my actions and so I proceeded with kindness and professionalism.

I once again have to give full credit to my parents for this.

Some of you may have heard the term "tiger mom."[6] A tiger mom is a parent who is strict and demanding of her kids, usually when it comes to education and sporting/musical abilities.

I wouldn't classify my mom as your typical tiger mom. While both Mom and Dad had high expectations of us, they focused their disciplinary actions more on being respectful and considerate kids as opposed to being straight A students. While they realize how important education is, they placed more emphasis on raising model citizens – kids who would strive to do the right thing over anything else; kids who were helpful, gracious, and grateful for everything they have in life. And that has helped me tremendously in how I have dealt with some of these micro aggressions and behaviors.

Of course, I'd have hoped that these situations would have been isolated incidents, but today, I am no longer that naïve. I've heard of these stories more often than I'd like to from friends in varying industries. The micro aggressions, blatant discrimination, and passive-aggressive behavior continue in many work environments. I have experienced them personally and watched them affect other minorities. I hear from friends in the industry how they have had to deal with similar issues. Again, these situations are completely unnecessary, but stereotypes and negative perceptions do happen.

---

6   Tiger mom - noun; a strict or demanding mother who pushes her child or children to high levels of achievement, especially by using methods regarded as typical of childrearing in China and other parts of East Asia; a tiger mother. *Lexico*, https://www.lexico.com/definition/tiger_mom.

Despite the complexity of the relationship with Daniella, I embraced this chapter in the Middle East by staying focused once again on the end game, reminding myself of the incredible opportunity to make a difference on a global scale. I held closely to my faith to help me get through all of the pessimism. I successfully completed my stint as an expat and cherish all the amazing adventures and memories. I am beyond grateful for my time in the international arena and for all the amazing friendships I acquired as an expat.

**"My whole life has been about changing negatives into positives. I got famous, then I got cancer, and now I live to talk about it. Sometimes the best gifts come in the ugliest packages." — Fran Drescher**

# CHAPTER 5

# KNOW YOUR JOB, DO YOUR JOB

## — Nick Saban

The year 2020 was an interesting one for all. It forced us to reflect on what's important to us, and for most of us in corporate America, it forced us to slow down a little. It also presented the opportunity to pick up new hobbies. Thankfully for me, I experienced more silver linings than I had anticipated.

Many people picked up baking and gardening and focused on home improvement. I have a client who with his bare hands built an entire back patio deck for his two kids; he assures me that this would never have happened if it wasn't for the time he saved by working from home due to the threat of COVID. Some of us picked up many great books that have been sitting on the shelf. I have been able to golf more since it is one of the more allowable outdoor activities. To my surprise, I also did my fair share of gardening. In March and April 2020 alone, I planted over 100 succulents, something I would never have done if not for the pandemic. My mom would be so proud of my gardening skills if she could see them.

Pre-COVID, I spent too much of my time in Los Angeles driving from one meeting to another, attending one industry event after another; it was taxing. These days I am also reading and watching more documentaries. I have even found the time to finally put my thoughts down on paper by writing this book.

Speaking of documentaries, I came across an HBO original featuring Nick Saban. The title of the documentary was *The Art of Coaching*.

Who is Nick Saban? Nick Saban is a football coach who has led several national championship titles. No college football coach has dominated the modern era like he has. He has been head coach of the (University of) Alabama Crimson Tide since 2007 and under his leadership, has led Alabama to five national championship titles. Impressive! It was 2:00 am and this documentary happened to be on. Being an athlete myself, I really enjoyed learning about what made Coach Saban and his team so successful and unbeatable. I love the spirit of competition and really admire individuals and teams that have won consistently while defying all odds.

In the documentary, Coach Saban explained that his teachings were to ensure everyone knew their role and position on the field. No matter what the position was, his instruction was to know your purpose and position at all times; to fully understand what you are expected to do, and then to do it in the best way you know how. When asked by the reporter about the most important advice he gave to his players, he would say to them, "Know your job, and then do your job." I found those words to be so simple and yet so powerful.

What a concept! Know your job, do your job. Know what is expected of you and then perform like your life is dependent on it. Coach Saban knew that once everyone embraced and bought into this philosophy then everything was achievable, and nothing could stop them. He was right! He was tenacious and held on to this philosophy, hence the five national championship titles.

History has shown us time and time again that women who made their mark in history and were ultimately trailblazers had several traits in common. They had a calling to make a difference and once they identified what they were passionate about, they stuck to it and did it well. They were relentless, to say the least. And to be relentless is to have tenacity. My mother had tenacity when she started her business at a time when it was uncommon for women to be entrepreneurs. The women who marched and created a ground level movement to allow all women to vote screamed tenacity.

I can't imagine living in a time when women are not allowed the privilege of voting. Where I grew up in Malaysia, I didn't have many female role models – sad, but true. My mom was the only one I looked up to. But we all know that regardless of the stereotypes and challenges with which we are faced, strong women do and accomplish impossible things every single day. Many, I know, overcome and achieve great things silently. It is always the women who make history who possess the skills required to accomplish something completely unbelievable. I believe this is because tenacity is a characteristic that sets these women apart, and one that we must nurture in one another to thrive, especially in today's world.

To be tenacious is to have an unwavering commitment to a position, principle, or course of action. Yes, optimism is great, and goal-setting is equally as important. Oprah Winfrey, a talk show host, media executive, author, actress, and billionaire philanthropist reminds us of that; she encourages all of us to have a vision board. Action plans are essential, and hard work is without a doubt necessary. To succeed in life and in business, we need all of these characteristics and more. But before any of them come into play, we have to know what we want and be tenacious enough to hold on to it. After all, I can't change the color of my skin, my slanted eyes, or the country where I was born, nor should I have to. Therefore, my lifeline is my ability to be tenacious and that tenacity has helped me to endure hardships that come in the form of unproductive relationships.

As an immigrant in America, I feel I have a duty to live up to — being a responsible and active contributor to society — and I take this privilege very seriously. Most immigrants I know take this very personally and approach it with great pride and responsibility. I've done so not just for the companies for which I have worked, but also for the communities in which I have lived.

In the fall of 2020 I heard through various friends of Asian descent who live outside of California, that when a lot of negative statements were being made about the COVID-19 pandemic and its ties to China, they had to pay the price for it even though they were first and second generation Asian Americans. Neighbors and friends who they once thought were their friends came into question. They started having to avoid going into the grocery stores at peak hours and started spending more time indoors and away from the general public for fear of being stared at and for fear of what could potentially happen to them and their families. Even in Los Angeles, I could relate to this scenario. I remember getting a few stares myself while walking into a grocery store one afternoon. This was before the full stay-at-home orders took effect and before masks were made mandatory.

These incidents caused me to reflect.

If it's one thing I've learned about my upbringing and about being Chinese and growing up in Asia, it is that I was raised and surrounded by individuals who exuded tenacity. My uncles and aunties spent so much of their time working so they could put food on the table for their kids. They were willing to do any job and multiple jobs to make ends meet. They did not have an education and would prefer to work every day, all day and night, than to beg for money or borrow from a relative. It's about pride, strength, and tenacity, and having these memories gives me the passion and drive that allow me to thrive in service of the community in which I live today.

Over the years, I have continuously stayed active by giving back. I have supported the Midnight Mission, an organization founded in 1914 that houses and provides for the Los Angeles homeless community, and have volunteered over the holiday season by serving breakfast to hundreds of homeless individuals looking for a hot meal. I have also volunteered with the California Hospital Medical Center (CHMC) Foundation, which supports the underserved Downtown Los Angeles community. In addition, I have participated in various fundraising events on behalf of the hospital. I am also thankful that I work for a company that allows me to continue giving back to the charities I believe in and is supportive of encouraging all employees to give back to their communities. Every year on September 11th, the company commemorates the passing of the founder by encouraging all employees to support a charity of their choice. The company makes a financial contribution to each charity based on the hours each team member has dedicated towards the activity. In 2020, employees of the Los Angeles team donated over 400 pieces of clothing to homeless hospital patients at CHMC through their foundation and a program called the Clothing Closet.

In today's world, where we are bombarded by so much chaos, fake news, and falsehood, I feel even more obligated now than ever to support the community I live in and to emerge as an Asian immigrant with a voice presenting a positive message. This is certainly not the time to be overshadowed by the things happening around us. Therefore, I am inviting all Asians and immigrants to rise to the challenge, to be tenacious, and to continue to do what we have always done, which is to support our local communities and to show our gratitude for the opportunity to live the American dream.

Why step up? The reason is that one of the best ways to turn a negative perception is by doing something good with our actions. Retreating from our communities is not an option. We must not allow our contribution to society to be buried or shrouded by darkness. On that note, we must not allow stereotypes to define us. As immigrants we have a duty to give back; therefore, we must do our part by being tenacious and by contributing with conviction.

Pulitzer Prize winner Viet Thanh Nguyen could have chosen to stay silent and not share his family's struggles and subsequent contributions, but he chose to share their story and he chose to speak up. Today, he garners a worldwide audience and when he speaks, people listen. He leaves a lasting impression by inspiring them with his words. He continues to use his platform to educate and share real-life stories, the sufferings but also the contributions of refugees in America.

One of the most common threads of going through the process of being stereotyped is being faced with a significant amount of passive-aggressive behavior. In the business environment, I found that when an individual needed my connections, he or she would have no qualms about asking me for an introduction to a client or a strategic partner. Beyond that, I experienced unsupportive, selfish, self-centered, and competitive behavior. In addition, as an Asian woman, one of the common stereotypes is that we are submissive. It is really easy to retreat when put into a position to have to deal with negativity or to harbor negative thoughts and to let the situation defeat us. It's too easy to just say "I'm not happy here" and then to second-guess who we are, our contributions, and our ability to thrive in the position. Women often blame themselves for just about everything. "Maybe

I could have approached this scenario differently. Perhaps I should have been more supportive," or "I could have positioned myself in the back of the room so no one would notice me." We are, after all, extremely creative creatures and can come up with some amazing excuses to not allow ourselves to be seen, heard, and understood. This is the "yin." Now let's focus on the "yang."

Again, tenacity is what allows us to stay focused and mission-driven. It is only knowing what we truly want that makes us as unstoppable as Coach Saban and his team of winners who exude that sort of mindset every time they set foot on the field. Thankfully today, I can say that I have accumulated a list of friends who have inspired and have challenged me to dream big and to continue to be fiercely tenacious. I will be introducing these individuals in the upcoming chapters. But before we move on, I would like to highlight an icon whose tenacity defined the future for millions and generations of women.

Talk about someone who knew her job and then did her job so exceptionally well!

Justice Ruth Bader Ginsburg (RBG) was an icon for justice. As the second woman appointed to the Supreme Court, RBG aimed to entirely change the law on gender equality. She inspired all of us every day to continue to push for diverse representation and equal pay, position, and parity. I hope her legacy lives on through all of us – both men and women. She was a tremendous leader who galvanized us all with support and we need to continue saluting her and saying her name. Her accomplishments were nothing short of extraordinary. As a young Jewish woman, she too faced a series of stereotypes. Her tenacity ultimately defined her success. She didn't allow the stereotypes to define her role, her grit, or her passion.

Her unbelievable and inspiring story starts in 1933, the year she was born. At a very young age she experienced the death of her sister and mother. She entered Cornell University on a full scholarship and during her first semester, she met her future husband, Martin ("Marty") Ginsburg, who was also a student at Cornell. Martin, who eventually became a nationally prominent tax attorney, was diagnosed with cancer. RBG had the responsibility of raising her first child while taking care of her husband as he battled the disease. She did all this while attending Harvard Law School. RBG eventually completed her legal education at Columbia Law School, serving on the *Law Review* and graduating in a tie for first place in her class in 1959.

Despite her excellent credentials, she struggled to find employment as a lawyer, because of her gender and the fact that she was a mother. At the time, only a very small percentage of lawyers in the United States were women, and only two women had ever served as federal judges. Thanks to her tenacity, her passion for what she believed in, and her increasing outspokenness, RBG became known as a prominent, progressive, and feminist hero. I can't even begin to imagine her struggles, the hard work, and the sacrifices she had to endure, and for those reasons and more we must not forget her contributions and those of other "sheroes" that came before us. She did not allow the stereotypes to define her and we shouldn't either.

Like many Asians I know, I have been faced with stereotypes most of my adult life and the micro aggressions are inevitable, but that doesn't mean I should allow them to take control of my life and influence who I am. Through all of my struggles, I've found the strength to stand up for myself. While it can be extremely scary, the effects of not doing so will ultimately define who I am as a professional and how others will treat me. What I want to encourage you to do is to use the stereotypes to harness your inner strength because it is your tenacity that will get you to your goals and to being your best authentic self.

In the process of discovering your best self, the stress that creeps into your life is going to be inevitable. Speaking from experience, I know how daunting and stressful it can be to have to either live up to a stereotype or denounce it, so I started to seek out what experts would recommend about managing negative environments. How do we in our journeys of navigating the yin and the yang find peace and balance in our crazy, busy lives?

I, like millions of other Americans, learned about Deepak Chopra by watching Oprah. Deepak Chopra is an alternative medicine expert and author of *The Seven Spiritual Laws of Success* and 80 other books. The self-help guru discusses the relationship between consciousness and health and how intimately connected the human body and spirit are as one unit. Much like the yin and yang, you can't have one without the other.

One of the most popular methods Mr. Chopra recommends for managing a negative encounter is the S.T.O.P. method.[7] What is it? Well, he encourages us to do this every time we are faced with a precarious situation:

S = Stop whatever you are doing

T = Take three deep breaths

O = Observe what's happening to your body

P = Proceed with kindness and compassion (my favorite part)

Why? As he reminds us – our health depends on it.

---

7    Sara Silverstein, "Deepak Chopra offers advice on how to manage stress and find meaning during the pandemic," *Business Insider*, April 22, 2020, https://www.businessinsider.com/deepak-chopra-managing-stress-finding-meaning-amid-coronavirus-pandemic-2020-4?r=DE&IR=T#:~:text=Chopra%20says%20when%20you%20feel,Proceed%20with%20awareness%20and%20compassion.

I sure wish I had known this in my 20's when I was starting out in a male dominated career.

In addition to implementing the S.T.O.P. method in our lives, he advises us that any successful collaboration requires three things: shared vision, an emotional and spiritual bond with the person or persons with whom you collaborate, and complementing each other's strengths. If you include those three ingredients, according to the self-help guru, it leads to a good recipe for any kind of partnership.

Mr. Chopra's teachings, methods, and success also reflect his tenacity. Born in New Delhi, India, he immigrated to the United States in 1970 and is described as "one of the top 100 heroes and icons of the century" by *TIME* magazine.

With all the recent protests in 2020 and 2021 for everyone's opinions and voices to be heard, I was also curious about how we as individuals can sustain our presence in service of others to help humanity in a society where judgment and fear run rampant, especially towards certain ethnic groups. I recall Mr. Chopra's approach on this.

The self-help guru reminds us that the first thing we need to recognize is our ability to learn to be independent of the good or bad opinions about us. Imagine that! What an amazing concept. He adds, if you're always at the mercy of other people's opinions, then, you'll never go anywhere. He encourages us to focus on our passion — to figure out what excites us, what our unique gift is — and then to simply give it away. The rest will happen as it should. I love this philosophy!

In many ways, the concept of this book is born from this very idea of sharing something I am passionate about with the hopes of making a positive contribution.

In Mr. Chopra's teachings, he encourages all of us to approach any negative stereotype or situation imposed on us with a "give-back" attitude – giving back to someone else with kindness and compassion, with a servant focus, by utilizing our voice and our actions. I am choosing to do this by being more proactive for the equality and empowerment of others, even if it means giving back with kindness and compassion to the individual who is at the root of the negativity. We have to learn how to navigate our personal journeys while being kind and sharing our unique gifts, whatever they may be. We have to be the first to step up, to be the bigger person, and become the driving force for any kind of change to begin. Only then can we start to lift each other up.

I have decided my contribution is to place my efforts and focus on creating an inclusive and diverse workplace. How? By implementing an equitable, welcoming and proactive recruitment strategy and by ensuring consistent and inclusive employee engagement happens at all levels. I will continue to support the team's professional and personal growth and will be their biggest cheerleader. I am thankful to work for a company today that allows me to actively lead and encourage these activities on its behalf.

We are often told that our peers and colleagues are our greatest assets. I whole heartedly believe in this philosophy. If we believe that training employees technically to succeed in their current positions is an important piece of the company's growth, equally important is that we must work to inspire them to improve their social engagement and networking skills in support of inclusivity and diversity for the company's future. This includes providing all employees with a platform to communicate and collaborate openly and effectively. I would love to see the construction industry as a whole work harder towards ensuring that all ethnicities and all women have opportunities and equality across all levels, in and outside of the boardroom, in the C-suite, in middle management, and at the project management/ support level.

If you are a minority woman, like myself, in a male dominated industry, I am sure you agree we have to be that much more intentional and supportive of our environment. How can one accomplish this? Continue to be that agent of change, be there for someone else, take the time to get to know your colleagues, ask questions with genuine curiosity, and help move the needle forward.

The construction industry in particular is an extremely dynamic, constantly evolving, fast-paced, innovative, and complex business. Therefore, in order to keep up with the changes, we have to take the time to understand other people's perspectives, while creating ways for our teams to work with greater collaboration and efficiency. Being self-aware combined with participation in team development activities will help all of us to improve on the relationships we encounter on a daily basis and will also automatically create an entire list of other positive characteristics, thereby optimizing a team environment for success.

As Coach Saban preaches there's nothing more important than knowing your job, then performing as a team. Can you envision an environment where inclusivity and diversity are at the optimum and everyone is working towards a common goal? I know I can!

Thankfully, the culmination of the stereotypes I have faced has helped me discover my passion, fueled my ambition, and revealed a path of endless possibilities. As a young girl growing up in Malaysia who knew exactly what was expected of her, which is to consistently excel in school, sports, the arts, and society, my upbringing has been the catalyst for my success today.

I knew my role and my job as a Chinese daughter and did what I could to the best of my ability to live up to those expectations.

My whole existence as a kid growing up in Malaysia was to stay out of trouble and to make my parents proud; those were the fundamentals with clear expectations. I have succeeded so far by staying out of trouble. I am hoping this book will make my parents proud.

**"As women, one of our greatest weaknesses is also one of our greatest strengths: being underestimated." — Sara Blakely**

# CHAPTER 6

# I REPRESENT INFINITE POSSIBILITY. PLEASE DON'T PUT A LIMIT ON MY POTENTIAL

## I did say please...

While I am grateful to and for Walter Sr. and Guy Mehula, who were kind enough to take me under their wings, in my 20's and 30's I never had a female mentor to help guide me in my decisions and in my career. I wished I had someone to confide in. I know life would have been a whole lot more manageable and enjoyable if I had someone to talk to and someone to help me make and navigate important career decisions. When I entered my 30's, I was determined to identify one or two female mentors and went out of my way to seek out other women from the industry who would be willing to serve as a role model. Unfortunately, I learned very quickly that they were few and far between and the ones I knew were too busy climbing the corporate ladder, too busy raising their kids, or too busy protecting their turf. Add to that, it was even harder trying to establish an Asian woman mentor. I simply could not identify an Asian woman from the industry to be my mentor. The deficit was real.

It is no secret that numerous studies have shown the lack of diversity of women in the design, engineering, and construction industry. According to an article issued by *Construction Dive* in 2019, of all the people who work in construction, women comprise only a small nine percent of the workforce.[8] In the last 10 years, that percentage of women in the industry hasn't changed. So, I started asking myself this question: how is this possible? We've made so many changes and advancements in inclusivity and have been consistently promoting women into leadership positions. The truth is, despite all of our efforts over the last 10 years, a significant number of women have likely hit the burnout rate, have chosen a different career path, or as an industry we haven't done a great enough job with employee retention. There is also the likelihood that women are not as supportive to each other as they could be. I know in my own experience, very few women were genuinely supportive of my trajectory.

Having been in the industry the last 15 years I wanted to better comprehend how other women feel about the industry today and if they feel the way I do about their experience as a female in the construction industry. I wanted to know how much more work needs to be done. I was also interested in this issue as I was in the midst of developing my message and theme as the incoming Asian American Architects and Engineers Association (AAa/e) President in 2021.

I wanted to explore how I could use my platform as President to inspire, empower and elevate women in a very male dominated industry.

---

8   Kim Slowey, "By the Numbers: Women in Construction," *Construction Dive*, March 6, 2019, https://www.constructiondive.com/news/by-the-numbers-women-in-construction/549359/#:~:text=The%20percentage%20of%20women%20in,%2C%20only%203.4%25%20were%20women.

The AAa/e is a non-profit organization founded in 1978 for the purpose of promoting and advocating for minorities who were underrepresented in the architecture, engineering, and construction industry. It is an organization that supports diversity, inclusivity, and equity, in which everyone is respected for their ability to contribute positively to society. AAa/e's mission statement reinforces its commitment to providing a platform for empowering professionals working in the built environment in personal and professional growth, business development, networking, and leadership in our community.

My role as President of the AAa/e organization gives me the opportunity and platform to feature and highlight women in leadership roles. It also gives me the platform to empower other women to join the industry. To better understand how women have evolved in this male dominated industry, I felt compelled to do some additional research, which included initiating a survey.

In November of 2020, I invited 100 women from the construction, design, and engineering industry in Southern California to participate in this anonymous survey. The participants ranged from middle to senior level executives. Some have been in the industry five years and others 20 years. The age range represented was 27 to 60. Respondents represented an array of specializations from within the industry with titles such as Program/Project Executives, Directors of Facilities Planning, Principal Architects, Directors of Construction, Marketing Managers, and Business Developers. Here's how they responded to the six survey questions:

**Question #1**

As a woman do you think your professional trajectory would be increased/elevated quicker if you were a man in the industry?

Yes or No

80% Yes, 20% No

## Question #2

As a woman in a male dominated industry, do you think other women have been supportive of your growth?

Yes or No

73% Yes, 27% No

## Question #3

As a woman in a male dominated industry, have you been ha-rassed, disrespected, de-valued and or belittled for being a woman?

Yes or No

77% Yes, 23% No

## Question #4

As a woman in a male dominated industry, have you been sex-ually or inappropriately harassed by another colleague/industry partner/client?

Yes or No

65% Yes, 35% No

## Question #5

As a woman in the construction industry, do you think more women could be supportive of each other?

Yes or No

97% Yes, 3% No

## Question #6

In line with identifying stereotypes, what are some of the most common stereotypes that come to mind about Asian women?

Please rate them by most common characteristic.

- #1. Asians are great at math
- #2. Asians are smart
- #3. Asians are bad drivers
- #4. Asians are submissive

I was surprised by the overwhelming responses to the survey. After completing it, the majority of the participants sent me a note on the side thanking me for asking these critical questions. I was even more pleased to know that the majority of respondents were my clients. I also appreciated their honesty and understanding regarding what I was trying to do for the construction industry as a whole.

Another revelation from conducting this survey was that I felt like as women we never discussed these issues as a group. We all know about these issues and that there is more we need to do, but I felt as if no one took the time to ask these women their opinion on inclusivity and equality in the workplace, how their experience has been for them, and how it has shaped who they are today. I was glad to see how responsive everyone was and how grateful they were that I asked these difficult questions.

It took me a month to process the results of the survey responses and after analyzing them I am convinced that this industry is capable of doing a lot more to change the landscape for all women. There is also more work to be done regarding how men can support equality in the workplace through the elevation and promotion of women. While the survey presented profoundly impactful observations, it also raised a lot of new questions.

When women and minorities lack representation in an organization, who then are their mentors? Who gives them a voice to be noticed and recognized? I would hazard a guess that all professional women know how awful it is to feel invisible in a room full of men. And if it hasn't happened already, I can almost guarantee that at some point in your career, someone will make you feel like your opinion doesn't matter even though you just shared a brilliant idea.

As women, we must start designing ways to encourage and retain more women in the industry. It starts with all of us – how we behave towards one another, and our recognition of each other's potential, because lip service simply doesn't get the job done.

Snubbing each other at industry events and conferences doesn't make it any better for anyone. About five years ago, I attended the American Society for Health Care Engineering (ASHE) annual conference. ASHE is an association dedicated to optimizing the health care built environment. It's one of the largest health care construction industry conferences in the country and attracts over 3,000 conference attendees. It's actually one of my all-time favorite conferences because it is a haven for networking. For three consecutive days we all get to see our friends from the industry and, more importantly, our clients from different health systems. The who's who from the industry usually shows up and it always ends up being an extremely memorable trip for all attendees because of the opportunities to run into our clients and partners at the many happy hour events, sometimes three to four hosted events a night, followed by a large party that usually ends around midnight and sometimes even later.

I do remember at this particular conference meeting up with industry partners on the first night. Most of the conference attendees always used the hotel lobby as the main place to meet before heading out to the different opening receptions/happy hour events. I was by myself and saw someone I recognized; we were both connected on LinkedIn and had dozens of mutual friends from the industry. We were both fairly successful and both worked for large international firms. She was based in Northern California and I was in Southern California. Her friends were my friends, so since my friends hadn't arrived in the lobby yet, I thought I would take the opportunity to go up to her to connect.

I said hello and introduced myself. I still remember the dress she had on – a really, really tight blue dress with absolutely no wiggle room. She wore these incredibly high, high heels. She was ready for the runway. She looked at me and then completely snubbed me. She proceeded to ignore me and when she saw someone else she knew, she quickly started a conversation with the other person. It took me a quick second to realize that I had just been snubbed by someone I hardly knew, and for no good reason. I had had only the best of intentions, which was to connect and say hello.

If you are wondering what being snubbed is, according to Vocabulary.com, "To snub is to ignore or refuse to acknowledge someone." Personally, my definition of snubbing someone is being rude.

I said to myself, *That was very kindergarten-like. I thought I was at a conference with industry professionals. Do adults in their 40's still act this way?* I quickly snapped out of it and waited near the lobby entrance for my real friends to show up.

I will never forget how this individual made me feel, but I am also thankful to know that that is not the example I would ever want to emulate. Based on this experience, she has shown me the kind of person she really is and clearly not someone I would want in my circle of friends. Once again recognizing the yin, I saw the yang.

If you have experienced this in your own professional encounters, raise your hand! I don't expect all of us to sit around and sing Kumbaya all day long, but I would like to see some level of respect, professional courtesy, and kindness towards one another. I don't think that's too much to ask of anyone, not the least from this particular individual.

Unfortunately, that wasn't the only time I have been snubbed. It's occurred several times that I can remember in my 15-year career, twice by women and twice by men. The most recent snubbing incident happened in November of 2020. I was at an American Institute of Architects (AIA) annual charity golf tournament and had arrived a little early so I could get some networking in before the shotgun start, something I typically do for all golf outings. This individual in question is someone I have known for over 10 years. We worked for competing firms and he saw me from a distance. On prior occasions over the years, he was always cordial and friendly to me, but at this tourney, he pretended like he had not seen me even though I was only five feet away. I realize I am petite by stature, but I know I was standing within his sight, so I walked up to him and attempted to say hello since I hadn't seen him since the COVID lockdowns in March. Despite my attempt to say hello and to be friendly, he quickly pivoted to someone else and started talking to them instead. I was perplexed by his behavior and without hesitation I proceeded to the breakfast bar to get a bite in before we had to tee off.

I don't think I will ever quite understand why certain people behave the way they do, but I know that I will not let that sort of behavior take over my day, especially right before a golf tournament.

Here's what I do know: you don't have to belittle, disrespect, or hurt someone to get ahead.

On all occasions I always held my composure, never allowing myself to react negatively towards bad behavior. It's just not worth it. When someone else tries to make me feel uncomfortable or tries to make me feel less worthy than they are, I remind myself they are dealing with their own demons and are just having a bad day. I usually excuse myself very professionally and wish them a great conference/golf day. Remembering what Mr. Chopra says, I will always proceed with kindness and compassion.

Today, I draw from several women whom I respect and admire. I decided that if I couldn't get one or two mentors, I would select 10 to 12 women who would inspire me in different ways.

One of the advantages to having multiple mentors is the continuous flow of information and energy to draw upon. I believe women in leadership roles have an amazing and long-lasting impact on other women. The interaction and sisterhood provide us with a platform to recognize our differences, the strength we offer each other, the variety in communication style, and the different approaches and strategies that exist within all of us. All this creates a healthy learning environment.

Today, I continue to grow and evolve because of the positive examples of a group of friends from my inner circle. These individuals consistently encourage, embolden, and inspire me to reach for the stars. They are my sheroes – Nancy Freelander-Paice, Barbara Scheidegger, Noreen Diaz, Patti Harburg-Petrich, Lisa Lepore, Jacinta Vythilingam, and Julie Owen.

Together, we have shared disappointments, dissected heart breaks, shed tears, celebrated promotions and birthdays, and discussed personal and professional challenges. We have collaborated, corroborated, and openly provided constructive criticisms as and when needed.

In business development and with all relationships, how we communicate is key to our success and understanding of others; this skill can accelerate the resolution of issues and provides for a safe space, so everyone is able to express themselves in a receptive, collaborative, and productive manner.

In an article written by communication expert Jim Rohn, "The 4 Building Blocks of Good Communication," he reminds us that "If you just communicate, you can get by. But if you can communicate skillfully, you can work miracles."[9]

When you snub someone, you are taking away the opportunity to have a meaningful conversation not just for them, but also for yourself.

Speaking of being a successful and skillful communicator, at this point, I'd like to recognize perhaps the most significant impact one individual has had on my entire professional career. This person has propelled my career to unbelievable new heights. He has been by far my most influential mentor and someone who saw my infinite potential. If you are from the construction industry, you've probably heard of him. His name is Joseph "Guy" Mehula. Most of us in the industry know him simply as Guy.

Guy was the Chief Facilities Executive at one of the largest school districts in the country – Los Angeles Unified School District (LAUSD). He held that position from 2002 to 2010 and under his leadership he led the second largest school construction program in the country. Guy and his team of construction professionals oversaw upgrades on 77 million square feet of buildings and the construction of more than 100 new schools in eight years, totaling $20 billion in school construction – not an easy feat accomplished under the scrutiny of a very political school district.

Prior to LAUSD, Guy achieved the rank of Captain during his 29-year career in the United States Navy, managing a number of large-scale global assignments. He served as Commander of the 30th Naval Construction Unit, a 9,000-person enterprise with 27 subsidiaries.

---

9    Jim Rohn, "Rohn: The 4 Building Blocks of Good Communication," *SUCCESS* (October 9, 2019), https://www.success.com/rohn-the-4-building-blocks-of-good-communication/.

After Guy retired from LAUSD, he was recruited by a large international firm. While at Parsons, he headed up the Global Buildings division and was later named President of its Middle East division. Under his tenure, Parsons Middle East achieved record sales growth and doubled in size to over 5,000 construction professionals.

I first met Guy as my client in 2007. The architecture firm I was representing was designing two school projects for LAUSD and it was my job to stay in communication with him and to ensure our architecture teams were performing to the district's expectations. When Guy retired from LAUSD and decided to join Parsons, he reached out to me and invited me to join him at Parsons as Business Developer. I was totally surprised and respectfully questioned the offer. My exact words were, "Why would I want to work for a boring engineering firm?" He laughed. By that time, I already had an established relationship with Guy and so I was able to be blunt and cut right to the chase. He said he felt I was underutilized and could be learning and doing a lot more for the industry. I hate to say this, but he was right. I continued to listen. He then assured me that as long as I worked with him and his team at Parsons, he would do his best to prevent me from ever being bored. Boy! Did he keep his promises! Once again, I called my mom in Malaysia to seek her advice and blessing.

Like a good Chinese daughter, I waited for the appropriate time, since she was in Malaysia and I was conscientious of the time difference. I said, "Mom, I have a new job offer to go work for a large international engineering firm." Her response was, "Is it a better position?" I said, "Well, yeah. It's a larger company with a significantly larger platform but also with much greater expectations." She said, "You know how to read, don't you?" inferring her philosophy that if you can read you can cook. How well you cook is up to you. I said, "Well, yeah, but it's for a construction management and engineering firm and I don't know the first thing about either." Her next question was "Will you be making more money?" I said, "Significantly more." She followed up with "So when do you start?"

And just like that, I embarked on the next big chapter of my career. Little did I know the next 3.5 years were going to be the best years of my professional life to that point.

Guy was astute and was a great judge of character. He knew what motivated me and he knew how to get the best out of me. He also knew I was a quick learner and with some guidance I could take on any assignment and see it all the way through. He knew he could always count on me and that my deliverables would be nothing short of perfect. I am not sure how he knew all that about me, but he did. My guess is he saw my potential and decided with the right platform and support, and with a lot of faith, I would somehow step up to the plate and flourish. Thanks to his faith and trust in me, I was able to unleash a whole new level of skill sets and achieved success not just personally, but also for the team I worked with, and for that I am eternally grateful.

Guy challenged me and at the same time he gave me a seat at the table. He consistently included me at meetings and asked for my opinion, knowing I would come to every meeting prepared with competitor analysis, an understanding of the political environment, intelligence on the stakeholders, and what the clients were most concerned about and expecting from their consultants. He knew I would come to every meeting prepared because I didn't want to disappoint him. And because he didn't treat me like an admin or an assistant, no one else did either.

Guy saw my infinite potential.

What made Guy a great leader was how he kept the team motivated. It didn't matter what position you held, he knew everyone's name and spoke to all of us with respect. Perhaps it was as a result of his military training. Regardless, he was humble in his approach; he stayed open-minded to new ideas and knew how to adapt and pivot when needed. He stayed flexible to changing needs and demands.

I enjoyed working under his leadership because he knew how to challenge me, and he kept raising the bar. He always dared me to achieve the impossible and that kept me motivated and excited about my pursuits. I enjoyed our strategy meetings and found so much fulfillment working for him. Guy was such a seasoned professional; he consistently asked all the right questions and would push back when he felt the need to. Guy understood what it took to win a contract and how to execute it well. He knew that if you hired the right people with the right mindset and you placed them in the right positions to let them do what they were hired to do, they would excel. His job as a leader was to ensure every team member received the support needed to be successful.

I was also always blown away by how well Guy understood the criticality and sensitivity of politics within an organization and how having the right business development strategy with an associated plan for each and every pursuit can position the firm for new levels of growth and profitability. He knew that the role of a business developer was beyond just networking and lead generation, and he ensured that I was exposed to all aspects of the process. This meant understanding and executing initiatives by utilizing proven techniques, a focused approach, and a tactical plan. He understood the need for mastering and implementing S.M.A.R.T. (Specific, Measurable, Attainable, Relevant, and Timely) goals on everything we did.

He did not put a limit on my potential, and he didn't allow me to put a limit on myself. Together we reaped the benefits of a successful partnership, winning countless numbers of new contracts together, locally, nationally, and then internationally. Unfortunately, he retired in 2019 – way too soon, if you ask me.

But his teachings will stay with me forever. His famous words were, "Stay focused on the pursuit and don't do anything that is immoral, unethical, illegal, or stupid."

Years after I started working for him, I asked him why I had been selected to join him at Parsons. He could have, after all, hired whomever he wanted as his business developer and had a sea of highly experienced candidates from which to choose.

For one thing, he said I was always at a networking event before anyone else. As a military man, Guy took punctuality very seriously. Once I started working for him, I noticed that for any industry event or team meeting, Guy was consistently on time. In fact, Guy was never late for anything. Secondly, he said that his observation of me was that I always followed up when I said I would. And I did. If it's one thing my parents taught me, it was to always do what you say you are going to do. He said when he was my client and tasked me with something, I always came back in a timely manner either with a response or with the information he needed, and he always appreciated that. I never hesitated when it came to asking for help or directing Guy to the right person for answers. Thirdly, he said I was always very professional and consistently in a good, upbeat mood. I am sure my parents would agree with that as well. They always told me that I was born smiling, hardly cried as a baby, and was pretty low maintenance overall.

Guy said he noticed I was always approachable and happy at every industry event at which he saw me, and he observed how comfortable I was, working the room by myself. I have to give my parents full credit for raising me this way; they always encouraged me to learn how to address others and how to ask for what I needed. Lastly, he also said he noticed I didn't struggle to start a conversation with someone I had just met and that I didn't only focus my time on clients at an event; I shared my time equally with everyone in the room, showing that not one person was more important than another.

It's important to note that both Walter Sr. and Guy shared a couple of leadership traits. One was that they always said thank you, even when you were just doing your job. You may have scheduled a meeting or set up a lunch appointment for them and even though it was part of what was expected of you, they always took the time to say thank you. Not only that, they did it in front of others – clients, strategic partners, etc. as a way to acknowledge your efforts. I always appreciated and admired them for that.

They also always empowered you to do your job freely but were also available to support you when you needed them. They always gave credit when and where credit was due. They never took the limelight and they always complimented the entire team even though it was their leadership that allowed for certain strategies and ideas to take place.

In addition, their humility was palpable. You couldn't feel an ounce of arrogance from either one of them, no matter how hard you tried. Walter Sr. didn't let the fact that he was a successful real estate mogul with a Bentley influence how he treated people, and Guy always addressed his team in a warm and personable way. It didn't matter if he was addressing a small group of people or an audience of 500. He was always approachable and would direct the focus on everyone else instead of his own accomplishments.

I miss Walter Sr. and Guy a lot!

Today I am blessed to have a variety of sources of inspiration and strength – men and women who are leaders, trailblazers, "sheroes," rock stars, superwomen… call them whatever you want, I continue to embrace them. Sometimes it only takes a few seconds to make a profound impact, and sometimes these relationships stay with us for days, years, and a lifetime. Let's have the one for all and all for one attitude and let's not forget to say THANK YOU every chance we get.

In the last 15 years since joining the very male dominated construction industry, I've taken the time to observe and appreciate a few very incredible women who have overcome hardships, broken records, and blazed trails – shattering glass ceilings and then taking their successes by actively giving back to others. Below is a list of women with infinite potential who have created impactful movements for generations of other women.

**Susan B. Anthony, Civil Rights Activist.** She campaigned against slavery and for women to have the right to vote. If it wasn't for her tenacity, women would probably be second and third class citizens today. I couldn't imagine a life where women would not be allowed to vote.

**Priscilla Chan, Pediatrician, Teacher, and Philanthropist.** Daughter of Chinese Vietnamese refugees. She is the first college graduate in her family. She attended Harvard University and received her medical degree from the University of California, San Francisco (UCSF). Chan pledged $4.6 billion to charities. She was the founder of the Chan Zuckerberg initiative dedicated to addressing society's biggest challenges in social justice, disease, and education committed to building a better future for everyone. She is wife to Mark Zuckerberg, the co-founder and CEO of Facebook, Inc.

**Michelle LaVaughn Robinson Obama, Attorney and Author of** *Becoming*. Married to the 44th President of the United States, Barack Obama, she was First Lady of the United States from 2009 to 2017. She moved from humble beginnings to First Lady and has used her voice and her platform to encourage young girls to dream big.

Her grace, intelligence, humility, and sense of awareness are what I admire most about the former First Lady.

**Iyanla Vanzant, Motivational Speaker, Best-selling Author, and Life Coach.** One of the country's most celebrated writers and public speakers, she's among the most influential, socially engaged, and acclaimed spiritual life coaches of our time and best-selling author of over two dozen books. I've read almost all her books and I appreciate how she uses words to empower us to find the beauty and the balance life has to offer. She speaks so eloquently about everything life presents – the challenges and victories – and why we should embrace every single moment of it.

**Kamala Devi Harris, Vice President and "Mamala."** Making history and shattering ceilings, Vice President Harris is the first woman, the first woman of color, the first Black woman to be elected Vice President. She was also the first woman and first black woman to be District Attorney in California's history, first colored woman to be California's Attorney General, and first Black and Asian American Senator. Today she represents 350 million Americans on an international platform. Regardless of your political preference, one must admit that she is a woman who has made history by defying all odds, having been raised by immigrant parents and succeeding despite the stereotypes she's had to overcome, the labels and names she's had to endure (including "monster" and "nasty").

At a local level, I draw from a team of women who have shared my ups and downs – those who have gone out of their way to promote and support me and have allowed me to dream my ridiculously big dreams. I call them my entourage, women on Team Dianne.

I want to encourage all of you to identify women leaders you respect, admire, and look up to so you can harness their positivity, leadership, and tenacity. I encourage you to follow the movements they are creating for the advancement of all women, because any kind of prejudice is a burden on the past, it terrorizes and clouds the future, and makes the present that much more unobtainable. Don't allow yourself to be stymied or bullied by a stereotype. Use your potential to create infinite possibility for yourself.

**"I allowed myself to be bullied because I was scared and didn't know how to defend myself. I was bullied until I prevented a new student from being bullied. By standing up for him, I learned to stand up for myself." — Jackie Chan, international Martial Artist, Actor, Stuntman, Filmmaker, Action Choreographer, and Singer**

# CHAPTER 7

# CREATE YOUR PASSION PLAN, ONE THAT MAKES YOU GET UP AND DANCE

I grew up dancing and at a very young age, started performing in primary school. I enjoyed dancing and learning the choreography and loved being on stage with my friends. At the age of six it was very typical in Malaysia to be enrolled in ballet class, and I always looked forward to doing endless numbers of plies. I enjoyed the discipline required, the synchronized timing of the arms and legs, and the tip toeing around with my friends in our tutus.

I miss being six. Everyone in the Lee family enjoyed music. I was raised around it. Both my parents, in their younger days, sang, danced, and performed at talent shows, and as a typical Chinese family, all the kids learned a musical instrument. Mine was the organ (similar to the piano). As an adult and well into my 40's, I continue to enjoy dancing but hardly do it as much as I'd like to anymore.

Dancing is such a great way to express how we are feeling – joy, happiness, jubilation, a feeling of accomplishment, a sense of gratitude, and sometimes victory. Dancing makes us happy! And sometimes when we are happy, we get up and dance!

More often than not, I do get asked the questions "Why are you so happy all the time? What makes you high on life?" My answer is easy: I have so many things to be grateful for, literally – my health; my safety, happy and healthy parents; a fun, loving, and happy dog; my faith and relationship with God, a wonderful group of core friends, and a successful career and job I truly enjoy. I am fortunate to work with a team of professionals who recognize my worth and my ability to do what I do best on a daily basis. And that's just naming a few things that I am grateful for. There's a whole other list of things I could add to complete an entire new chapter.

I do, however, recognize the significance and relevance of the questions. Chances are, the person asking me those questions, is asking themselves what makes them happy or why they aren't happy or feeling fulfilled. And perhaps why they are in the predicament in which they currently find themselves. I respect the question and acknowledge that everyone is on a personal journey, a path of their own filled with twists and turns and with many unpredictable obligations and circumstances.

Whatever your circumstance, I want you to consider dusting off those dancing shoes. Please allow me to explain further. Perhaps you are long overdue for a night out, I know these days with the pandemic, many of us are feeling that way. Somehow you are going to have to find a way to continue dancing, even if that means dancing in your living room with the lights dimmed all the way down and your kids, husband, partner, or even your dog as your dance partner. I must admit, in the last 18 months or so I've had to do that several times with Ash, my five-year-old Blue Heeler rescue, especially since COVID has forced us into self-isolation. If you are not getting up to dance (metaphorically) at least several times a month, you are probably not living your best life. If this resonates with you, then it may be time to find a different dance partner aka job, find a different deejay aka boss, or find a new pair of dancing shoes aka passion.

My brother Alan loved music, he loved playing music, and dancing to it, and he enjoyed spreading the joy of music with everyone around him. I have never met anyone who was more obsessed with music than my brother. In 2010, the music we were accustomed to listening to as a family came to an abrupt end. While dining one night with his friends, Alan was killed by a driver who swerved into him.

Malaysia's tropical weather is extremely conducive to outdoor dining and most of the restaurants offer patio seating as an option. The best of Malaysia's food isn't served at fancy restaurants, but at stalls set up by the roadside, in hawker centers, or in street-side coffee shops. Hawker stalls and street food are found all over the country, in every neighborhood from urban sites to major cities, and even next to busy highways. Basic tables and stools are provided on-site, making this dining experience a unique piece of the Malaysian culture.

Unfortunately, on April 26th, 2010, my brother was taken from us in a senseless and tragic accident. He was sitting at one of those restaurant patios enjoying dinner with his friends, just a couple of miles away from home, when a car ran into him and killed him instantly. According to the autopsy report, the impact punctured his chest bones and lungs. We were told that the force of the impact was so severe that he never saw it coming or felt the point of impact. Alan was 46 when he passed and the only son in a Chinese family, which meant we were no longer able to carry the Lee family last name forward. I remember receiving the call from my father in Malaysia. Shortly after, I jumped on the first flight home out of LAX, a 21-hour journey, and arrived three days later (Malaysia is 16 hours ahead) on April 29th — my birthday — to bury my brother.

My brother's death was such a tragedy that it was splashed across the front page of every newspaper in Malaysia. The day after I arrived from Los Angeles, while still jet lagged, confused, and barely awake, I woke up to my mom showing me the newspaper articles that included pictures of the crime scene, detailing how my brother was randomly killed by a 27-year-old driver who was impaired. Those disturbing images will stay with me forever.

As a younger sister, I am so grateful to have witnessed my brother live his best life. Alan spent most of his time doing what he enjoyed and loved most – surrounding himself with music that he could sing and dance to. Alan played the drums, the harmonica, the guitar, and the organ. He did what brought him joy. He was dancing even when he wasn't moving his legs.

His love for music was evident even at a young age. He was in the school marching band and would return from school to listen to more music. We always knew Alan was home in his room because we could hear the music piercing through his bedroom door. My brother introduced me to many genres of music, from blues to country, rhythm and blues to rap, pop, and Top 40. He loved a variety of styles and had an eclectic collection of music from artists such as Dolly Parton, Hall and Oates, and Elton John; from Madonna to Tina Turner, Beatles, and Earth Wind and Fire, there wasn't an artist he didn't enjoy listening to.

Music was his true love, and he spent every waking moment immersed in it. And my parents did a phenomenal job fueling his passion. They bought him his first jazz set and his first guitar, and fully supported his enthusiasm for anything related to music. My parents even converted the entire back room into a music room just so Alan and his friends could have their jam sessions. I have fond memories of his friends coming over and the music they used to play together; it was great!

I applaud my parents for being so encouraging. In traditional Chinese families, boys are usually expected and encouraged to be an accountant, a doctor, or a lawyer. Sometimes, they are even expected to achieve two of these three professions. But my parents didn't allow that sort of stereotype to define Alan's future.

And because of that, Alan never stopped dancing. He lived his life to the fullest!

Unfortunately for my mom, shortly after Alan's death, she had to plan two additional funerals, all within an eighteen-month period. We lost two of her beloved brothers, Uncle Ken and Uncle Ku, within months of each other. Both uncles helped raise me and both played significant roles in my upbringing in Malaysia.

As I reflect on the tragedy from April 26th, 2010, what was more heartbreaking than grieving the loss of my brother was having to watch my parents grieve the loss of their firstborn and only son. They say no parent should ever have to bury their children and what I witnessed was definitely an unexplainable deep sense of devastation. Losing a child is a life-changing experience and the unexpected tragedy weighed heavily on all of us. The first few years after Alan's death were the most difficult; for years I wouldn't allow myself to celebrate my birthday. The guilt of celebrating my birthday on the day he was buried just didn't sit well with me.

I share my family's loss not to garner sympathy, but to let you know that my brother lived his life the way it made him happy and he didn't succumb to peer pressure, family expectations, or a stereotype. My goal for myself is to do the same. And it's something I hope for you.

From this experience, combined with the tragic number of deaths 10 years later, in 2020 and into 2021, I am reminded of how much human suffering occurs in the world. However, I am also encouraged by the will of the human spirit. Our ability to endure, survive, and come out stronger despite all of the affliction and hardships is admirable and inspiring. The human spirit gives us the capacity to dig deeper, far beyond our imagination.

Unfortunately, I have a long list of friends who are simply going through the motions at work, and are often just making it work. For them, I pray that they find fulfillment and happiness in other ways if not from their careers.

Often times, some level of disruption has to occur for growth and self-development to take place, and that requires some form of risk. I am taking a risk by sharing my life's story with all of you and I hope through my lessons learned and struggles, I can help turn moments of uneasiness into opportunities for self-improvement for all of us.

The reality is we will never be able to control how much time we have on earth. We are also unable to control how other people perceive, judge, or treat us, but what we can do is redirect any kind of negativity we receive by doing something good and kind. I suggest doing this by channeling all that negative energy into doing something good for someone else. We can always do something to shift the negative into a positive, and this method automatically creates a healthy distraction.

Your positive actions can be directed to an individual or a group of people; it could be for someone you know or for a perfect stranger. The key is to channel all the frustration and negative energy into doing something kind and generous for someone else. Regardless of the gesture you choose to carry out, be sure to do it the best way you know how and with grace and benevolence. Remember what

Coach Saban said: "Know your job, do your job." Even with the act of kindness, whatever you choose it to be, do it with authenticity and altruism. Know that you have the power to control how you want to react to a situation.

On the upside, I've also met many women in their 30's and 40's who have drummed up the courage to listen to their passion by starting their own businesses so that they can be in charge of their own destiny, and that's extremely admirable. As women, we now live in a time where anything is truly possible, with or without the stereotypes imposed on us, and that's reassuring for all of us.

I am grateful that I have found peace in this dog-eat-dog world and that I am given the opportunity to utilize my skill sets to advance growth for the firm I represent. It is extremely fulfilling to work for a company that values my contribution and to work with a group of professionals who see me for who I am.

It was a real honor to have the front row seat to my brother's life, and his death is a reminder of how precious our time is and how critical it is for us to identify our passion so we can continue to dance more than just a few times a month. Don't let an obstacle or a stereotype define your future, your worth, your life, and how you spend your time. Take the time to discover who you are so you too can get up and dance. Most of all, don't settle for being mediocre.

I am declaring 2021 as the year for real change to take place. Let's collectively make a conscientious effort to elevate each other. My hope is to shift the percentage (9%) of women currently in the construction industry to over 15% by 2025. Yes, it's an aggressive goal and I welcome the challenge. Will you join me? In order to accomplish this, there has to be a concerted effort and an acceptance of a new way of approaching things. As women, it starts with us. We must want to choose to inspire, empower, and catalyze diverse yet like-minded individuals, agencies, and organizations to help all women realize their full potential. We need to continue creating meaningful connections, be a resource to others, and rally the support of all women in order to ensure success.

We must continue to lift and celebrate each other.

So how can we collectively accomplish this?

We can start by embracing the right mindset of giving, caring, and sharing, followed by having some simple actionable next steps. Below I share what I am suggesting our call to action should be. Select one or two or three but start something today.

What is our call to action?

- We can start by not snubbing each other.
- Listen to each other more.
- Continue to highlight women in leadership roles, trailblazers.
- Share learning opportunities – technical or non-technical.
- Stay relevant and present in the industry by making your voice heard.
- Offer to support other women.
- Help change the company culture, create a culture of inclusivity.
- Develop a new generation of women.
- Volunteer to be a mentor.
- Join an industry organization so you can contribute meaningfully.
- Introduce yourself to the girl in the corner.
- Put on your dancing shoes.

Why is this important? It's important because action leads to change.

My call to action is to continue promoting the benefits of diversity and inclusivity. I am using my platform as President of the Asian American Architects and Engineers Association (AAa/e) to feature women in leadership roles and the value they bring to the construction industry with the hopes of attracting a new generation of diverse women. We all know that the benefits of bringing a diverse talent pool to any industry are limitless. We know that the inclusion of different people based on gender, race, ethnicity, and sexual orientation is a business advantage. Companies that prioritize diversity are outperforming others; they are seeing greater earnings, better governance, more thoughtful innovation, and overall better morale. If we can all focus on intentionally recruiting a more diverse workforce, we would all have a hand in creating a more united, productive, and peaceful environment in and outside of the office.

As the 2021 President of the Asian American Architects and Engineers Association, here is my message and my pledge:

*It is with honor and privilege that I assume the position of President of this great association in 2021. I would like to applaud and express my gratitude to all the Past Presidents who have come before me. Without them AAa/e wouldn't have the reputation, the brand recognition, and most importantly the respect of the entire construction industry.*

*I have identified three objectives that are near and dear to my heart:*

*#1. To continue to be the organization of choice that delivers up-to-date information on capital improvement programs; an organization that provides direct access to public agency owners, and a place for professional and personal education, mentorship, networking, and growth.*

*#2. As the past program chair for 2019 and 2020 I have challenged the incoming program chair to host a series of women in construction webinars. I am encouraging the committee to seek out women in construction in leadership roles representing various markets from aviation, health care, education, public agencies, and transportation. There is without a doubt a lack of representation of women in the industry and it is my personal goal to enhance their contributions and to give them a voice.*

*#3. As AAa/e continues to grow its member base, we will capitalize on our platform to transform our community and industry by welcoming a more diverse and inclusive group of industry professionals. We must advocate a culture that promotes diversity, equity, and inclusion by actively attracting new members regardless of gender, race, religion, age, or other factors.*

*As an organization we have a tremendous responsibility and a platform to represent the best of humanity. Everyone has a role to play in conquering this pandemic – the rise of racism and inequality. Now is definitely the time to address these issues. We want to be the kind of organization that is an example of the leadership the nation should want to emulate. Yes, all of this will impact how we do business and will forever change our industry, but I am confident that AAa/e will continue to stay focused on what the industry needs and how to best serve our loyal members. The goal is to propel us forward, not just for women, but as an entire industry and community.*

*I am hopeful that we will find common ground and that we will continue to harness what this community is best known for, which is good, old-fashioned ingenuity, resilience, hard work, innovation, and compassion, which we have consistently shown in challenging times. Like the rising phoenix that emerges from the ashes, we will emerge from this together, stronger, and better.*

*Thank you.*

I am honored to serve as President of this great organization and am fortunate to be able to bring together my passion for a specific mission.

This is where being passionate helps. If you are passionate about what you do, you will inevitably want to do it well and the results are often rewarding. Life may not always be the party we hoped for, but while we are here, we should identify our reasons to get up and dance to celebrate our victories. So, press on with pride, purpose, power, and passion. Now, let's put these actions into motion. Dust off those dancing shoes and I'll see you on the dancefloor.

**"If you're always trying to be normal you will never know how amazing you can be." — Maya Angelou, American Poet, Bestselling Author, Memoirist, and Civil Rights Activist**

# CHAPTER 8

# NAVIGATING UNWANTED ADVANCES

What I am about to share are real stories from the last 10 years revealing my not-so-pleasant experiences as a woman in a very male dominated industry. So as to not embarrass the four individuals I am about to reference in this chapter, I will for the sake of protecting their identities only refer to them by their initials.

The next few pages are some of the most uncomfortable situations of my professional career. The experiences are very real, based on facts, and some would call this the juiciest part of the entire book. You're probably wondering why I am choosing to protect these men's identities and the reason is simple, they are, as far as I know, still married, with kids and in some cases grandkids. They are still in the construction industry today. I don't consider them real threats, rather men being men and perhaps they had a moment of weakness, got too comfortable, and overstepped their boundaries with me.

Being a woman in the construction industry has made me more conscious and sensitive as to how I am perceived, especially in a business development/sales role, so I would intentionally go out of my way to always act and present myself professionally. I made an effort to remain approachable and friendly but never flirtatious. I always knew where the fine line was and habitually surrounded myself with respectable individuals. And even with that level of caution and professionalism, I've had to deal with sexual and inappropriate advances.

This chapter is not an attack on men. Its purpose is to bring attention and awareness as to how as women, we can continue to achieve our goals by staying focused on the business objectives and by being smart about handling uncomfortable situations.

As a reminder, here is how the women from the survey responded to these two questions:

## Question #3

As a woman in a male dominated industry, have you been harassed, disrespected, de-valued and or belittled for being a woman?

Yes or No

77% Yes, 23% No

## Question #4

As a woman in a male dominated industry, have you been sexually or inappropriately harassed by another colleague/industry partner/client?

Yes or No

65% Yes, 35% No

The results are a clear admission of what women go through and my personal experience is indicative of the reality we have to face.

Despite these high percentages, we can manage and overcome these inappropriate advances. How? By maintaining a heightened level of professionalism and respect for ourselves. We can continue to define our boundaries and use some basic common sense. This is where self-awareness, composure, and courage will help you get through some of these awkward sexual and inappropriate encounters. As women, regardless of your title or position, these incidents can happen.

In 2014 and 2015 I had the unfortunate experience of two incidents.

I had a great professional, positive relationship with my colleagues and as part of my position in business development was asked to attend a national aviation conference in Texas with the aviation team. There were seven of us in total; we were the who's who of the company – executives and directors who represented the firm.

On the first evening, upon arriving at our hotel, we had planned on meeting for dinner as a group, especially since we had all flown in from different parts of America to attend the three-day conference. One of the project directors named MT asked that I swing by his hotel room to meet up with him prior to meeting up with the rest of the team. It was a pretty typical request. MT had been with the company for a few years by then and I had communicated with him prior via email and at other in-person team meetings, so he wasn't a stranger to me.

We had planned on meeting as a group at the hotel lobby at 6:30 pm. Since I had just arrived from the airport and had just checked into the hotel, I didn't get the chance to really freshen up or change and was dressed in jeans with a top and a blazer. By that time, I was also starving and was ready to sit down with my team to enjoy a big Texan meal.

Being my punctual self, I knocked on his hotel room door a little after 6:00 pm. He invited me to come in because he said he had to put on his shoes. I wasn't worried; we were there to attend a work con-ference and after all, we were colleagues working for the same com-pany. He was nice and very cordial. I mean he wasn't at all creepy. He then insisted that I look around since he was in a suite and not a regular room, and part of that tour included a look at the bedroom. At this time, he was still walking around barefoot. He didn't even have his socks on. He then suggested I take off my heels so I could lie down next to him on the bed. Of course, this is when he started to get really creepy.

In fact, I think my exact words were "Why would I want to do that?" He continued to try to coerce me while sitting on the bed. His shoes were nowhere near in sight. He then reminded me we had a few minutes to kill and I should consider lying down next to him so we could relax together. I wasn't about to fall for that and at that point, I told him I would see him at dinner and walked myself out of his extra-large hotel room. As I left the room and made my way down to the lobby, I felt a sense of disgust and repulsion. *What was he thinking?* I asked myself. Needless to say, I was extremely disap-pointed by his behavior and his lack of respect for me as a colleague.

That was certainly not how I had envisioned starting this three-day conference. MT did a great job avoiding me for the next three days and I never heard from him or ran into him at the conference. He managed to somehow stay clear of me in the sea of 1,000 people. Thankfully, my position didn't require me to work directly with him, so we had very limited interaction from that time on.

Looking back, I also realize I was extremely lucky the incident did not escalate further and that I was quick to react by removing myself from what could have been something far more intolerable and serious. If you are curious about how the rest of my evening went, well, MT never showed up for the team dinner that night and

I learned about his abrupt resignation five months later. I also heard from several other colleagues that MT was notorious for hitting on multiple women, especially women with whom he interacted on a daily basis on the job site. Now, if I had known that that was his reputation, I wouldn't have agreed to enter his hotel room that evening in Texas.

A year later, I was casually conversing over text with a project director named SD. SD was a family man. He claimed he was happily married, with two daughters in college. He spoke fondly of his daughters and was proud of their athletic abilities. He was what I thought to be a decent man, a great project director, a team player by all accounts and very much an accomplished and seasoned professional. When I met SD he was just about to kick off a $500 million plus construction project and I had already known him for six months when what he said via text message changed our friendship forever.

We were texting about work when I informed him I was scheduled to be out of the country and that I was actually taking some time off. Naturally, he asked where I was headed. I said I was looking forward to my vacation in Belize. It was a snorkeling and yoga retreat and a vacation I had been planning on taking for quite some time. To my surprise his next text said, "May I see your tan lines when you return from your vacation?" I couldn't believe what I was reading, but also knew that sometimes things are often said in good fun, so I didn't respond immediately but before I could think of an appropriate response, I received another text from him. This time his text implied that he was interested in seeing certain areas of my bikini lines. Now, I was starting to get really agitated and offended. Did he think that little of me? Had I not acted as a professional the last six months? I was extremely surprised that he thought the text messages he was sending me were appropriate and that asking me to show him certain areas of my tan lines was acceptable.

I asked him why he thought it was OK to ask that of me. His response was that it wasn't a big deal and he thought it would be great to see what my bikini lines looked like. I paused and then said, "I wonder how your wife and daughters would feel if they knew this was how you were speaking to me, a colleague." He was clearly upset by my comments and started referring to me as being too sensitive, adding that he thought we were "real friends."

I reminded him that we were colleagues, and his requests were inappropriate and, frankly, quite disrespectful.

A few text messages later, he turned angry and started badgering me the next few days with nasty text messages instead of apologizing like a real man would have. After a few weeks, he stopped sending messages and I have never heard from him since, which I consider a real blessing. What I thought was a respectable and professional friendship between two colleagues was clearly not as it seemed.

I am not sure if there was anything I could have done to avoid this incident, but what I am sure of is that I will not tolerate or entertain such inappropriate and unprofessional requests.

As a business developer, pre-COVID, I used to attend a long list of industry conferences, luncheons, events, banquets, etc. On average I attended six to eight conferences a year and multiple breakfast, lunch, and dinner events every week. In addition, because I serve on several industry boards, I consistently attended board of director meetings several times a month. On an annual basis, certain organizations host annual awards and fundraising galas. I am passionate about what I do and enjoy getting together with other industry professionals. Networking is such a big part of what I do as a business developer.

It was the fall of 2014, my first year back in Los Angeles from Abu Dhabi, UAE. I had completed my international assignment with Parsons and was getting back into the Los Angeles market. I remember attending a premier industry gala in a beautiful and historic hotel in Downtown Los Angeles. There were over 400 industry attendees. Anyone and everyone from the industry including public and private clients attended this gala every year. It attracted the who's who from the construction industry. Men would be dressed in tuxedos while some women wore beautifully selected gowns. Most of us showed up right after work in cocktail dresses and some in perfectly tailored suits accompanied by beautiful accessories. I wore a long-sleeved dress that came to the knee. I still remember the dress I wore; it was a dark blue, round neck Ted Baker dress with pretty and colorful printed flowers that I had purchased in Dubai. In the interest of full disclosure, it wasn't one of those body-hugging tight dresses; it was a full coverage A-line dress, both pretty and dressy enough for the occasion. My heels were no more than three inches high.

I attended the gala with one of my best friends, Taylor, who is an engineer in the industry. We planned on arriving together around 6:00 pm for the networking and knew that would give us 90 minutes – ample time to enjoy the networking before the actual program started at 7:30 pm. At around 7:15 pm the bells started ringing and the lights started to dim, so everyone started to make their way into the dining room. We started looking for our table and grabbed our seats in the beautifully decorated room and promptly sat down as the program started.

I was pleased to have been randomly seated next to a potential client, someone who has been in the industry for 25+ years, with an extensive network. This was someone who worked for a prominent and established private education institution. He served on several industry boards and we shared a long list of mutual friends and acquaintances. Basically, everyone he knew, I knew.

KN was someone I had known for over five years, so it was nice to reconnect with him at the banquet. He always touted himself as a strong Christian man and was a committed weekly churchgoer. KN was married and had two kids. Taylor was seated to my left and KN was seated to my right. There were seven other people at our table.

The gala started by recognizing several industry leaders and around 8:30 pm there was a 15-minute break. As everyone started to enjoy their dinners and the second round of networking began at the tables, all of a sudden, I felt a hand rubbing my right leg, just slightly above my knee. At first, I wasn't even sure if what I was feeling was real. I thought to myself, *Could it be?* Then I felt it again, and it occurred to me that KN was rubbing his hand on my knee under the tablecloth. My reflex had me turning to my right and at that very moment we locked eyes. I was immediately taken aback and moved my chair a few inches away. I had a few seconds to decide what my next move was going to be. In a matter of seconds several options crossed my mind. I could, like in the movies pick up the glass of wine sitting next to KN and splash him with it, embarrassing him in front of everyone at the table. I could have confronted him and said something like "Take your hand off my leg!" and then kicked him really, really hard under the table. I could have just sat there with his hand on my leg and pretended like I didn't feel anything or worse, pretended like I was enjoying his hand stroking my knee.

Instead, I leaned over to Taylor and said very quickly with a smile, that I had to leave and thanked her for hanging out with me. I got up from my chair, grabbed my purse, excused myself, and left the table, the room, and the banquet, never to return. I was completely disgusted by what I had to endure and have never conversed with this individual since.

Even though he was a potential client, I don't regret my reaction to the situation and certainly don't regret not having him as a client.

What would you have done if you were in my shoes?

The last story I am about to share is far more vocal and in the face. It involves a client from 2016. For the purposes of this book, again, I will refer to him only by his initials: DK. DK was in his early 50's, a successful developer and project executive in the Los Angeles area. He was married with two teenagers, a boy and a girl. By all accounts he was a great family man, totally dedicated to his kids and their many activities. He was smart and good-looking and enjoyed golf.

At that time, my pre-construction team was providing some preliminary services to his company and I had brought this new account to the firm. It was my job to maintain the client relationship. Eight months into the new account, one afternoon after lunch, DK brought up the fact that he wanted to know if I would consider being more than just a professional friend. I was really surprised by the suggestion and didn't want to make any assumptions and I responded by asking, "What do you mean?" He proceeded to tell me how attractive I was and that he was really attracted to me. He continued to share that he hadn't had an intimate relationship with his wife in over two years and was curious if being intimate with him was something I'd be interested in.

Mind you, all this happened with absolutely no one around us. We weren't at an event with people around; it wasn't a text message conversation I could stare and cringe at, and it wasn't a phone conversation I could place on mute to scream. It was in broad daylight, after leaving a restaurant on our way to our respective cars. There was simply nowhere for me to hide. I couldn't even hide my facial expression. I had to maintain my composure, my professionalism, and hide the disgust on my face regarding how he had clearly crossed the line. I smiled and said very politely, "That's really not something I would be interested in." Of course, without hesitation he came back with a response: "Why not?"

"For starters," I said, "I like to keep my professional and personal life completely separate, especially with a client relationship." I was hoping the conversation would end there and that it would never come up again. Instead, within seconds he came back with the most clichéd of all clichéd comments: "Don't you believe in friends with benefits?" At this time, I started to feel really uncomfortable. I didn't know what to do with my hands. Thankfully, I had my purse to hang on to for some level of comfort. Without hesitation, I said, "Well, you are a client and that would ruin the professional relationship I've worked so hard to establish." Before he could rebuke me again, I went on to say that if we crossed the line, it would change the entire dynamic of our working relationship. He looked at me with disappointment. He reluctantly accepted my reasoning. I maintained my professionalism and we said our goodbyes and went on our separate ways. Because he was an existing client, I was trying to keep the mood as comfortable as possible and was trying to avoid the awkwardness around the topic of the conversation.

A couple of days after that incident, I heard from him again, this time via several text messages. The message said he wanted to know if I had given more thought to his suggestion. Yes, he used the word "suggestion." I said not really. He then retaliated and insisted I was being too rigid about the whole thing, and that I should loosen up. Again, he brought up the friends with benefits concept and said he didn't quite understand why that was a big deal-breaker for me. He even said it's something everyone does, and he didn't understand why this was an issue for me. At this point, the entire text exchange was just beyond inexcusable and unbecoming.

And here's the kicker: as if I wasn't already uncomfortable about having to respond to him to defend my decisions, he said something that really irked me. "I thought you would be more submissive than that." Once again, even though this was said over text, I had to maintain my composure. Basically, I had to choose not to lose my XXXX. I politely responded, "Well, like I said before, I don't mix professional business with personal, and I hope you can respect that." This time, of course, I had the luxury of making all sorts of facial expressions to react to what I was reading and dealing with. I emphasized again that crossing that line would really hurt our professional relationship and that I respected him and myself too much to jeopardize the working association we had. I reiterated my hope to continue working with him as a client and politely said goodbye. Thankfully, the conversation ended somewhat well and although DK is not an existing client today, I walked away from the situation feeling a sense of relief and accomplishment, knowing that I had stood my ground and that I did what was right for me and the company I represented.

There is no doubt in my mind that similar situations have occurred to some of you and in some way shape or form, my stories have resonated with you. The survey results from November 2020 confirm that even amongst the women I know from the industry, over 65% admitted to being sexually or inappropriately harassed by a colleague/industry partner and/or client at some point in their career.

If you have had to deal with these uncomfortable and unwanted advances and have come out swinging, I want to applaud you for standing your ground and for handling it in your own unique way. I am convinced that some of you have had to deal with much more intense and precarious situations and my personal stories are probably mild compared to what you have had to go through and for that, I sympathize.

The reality is that these sexual advances will continue to happen but it's how we handle the situation that allows us to maintain our integrity and the respect we deserve. As women, these advances may happen to you and my desire is that you will never find yourself in these situations but if and when you do, I hope you will be able to have the courage to stay true to your core values, because what you do and how you react does matter. Stick to your guns to maintain your integrity and to protect your reputation. We will all react to these situations, relationships, and pressures very differently and my hope is regardless of how you choose to handle the situation, your number one priority is your safety and your overall emotional and physical well-being.

**"This world belongs to all of us, and all sexes should be able to live in respect and harmony." — Michelle Yeoh, international Malaysian Actress (*Memoirs of a Geisha, Crouching Tiger Hidden Dragon, Crazy Rich Asians*)**

# CHAPTER 9

# TURNING DISRESPECT INTO RESPECT FOR YOURSELF; THESE ARE MOMENTS THAT DEFINE YOU

Pulitzer Prize-winning author Viet Thanh Nguyen boldly and eloquently shares his parents' struggles and their story as refugees. He speaks to how his parents were disrespected in their new community upon arrival in California in the 70's, after being forced to flee Vietnam at the end of the Vietnam War.

Viet was only four years old when he and his family fled from war-torn Vietnam for a new life in America. Unfortunately, as his parents tried to build a business, they were "unwelcomed" by a sign in a nearby store that said, "Another American driven out of business by the Vietnamese." I can't even begin to imagine the stereotypes they've had to overcome and the sacrifices they've had to endure to be accepted into society. Today, Viet is using his platform to turn all of that disrespect into respect for himself and his family.

Stereotypes can and often do lead to racism. I am a business developer in a $1.3 trillion industry that is currently facing a historic labor crisis. Simply put, the construction industry cannot afford to shun anyone who wants to take on these challenging construction jobs. Just as important are the women who play critical roles in the management of projects – construction and project managers, project controls managers, engineers, architects, superintendents, and support staff. The construction industry is in desperate need of more resources. I know this because we are all competing for the same resources and this trend has been going on for the last 10 years. As an example, I work for a company that provides program, construction, and project management services, and we are consistently competing against other firms for the same technical resources. Individuals with education and Division of State Architect (DSA) experience and those with Office of Statewide Health Planning and Development (OSHPD) experience are highly sought after.

It's amazing how quickly we have to react as a team to identify qualified individuals, interview them, and then make the offer before they get swooped up by our competition. Just ask my talent acquisition manager. It truly is an employees' market.

Having to work through this, the industry as a whole cannot afford to have anything work against it. We must have strategies in place to help attract and retain the talent we need to sustain the growth of this demanding industry.

One of the ways to accomplish this is to have a clear path towards systemic change. Stereotypes and incidents of racism can have a destructive impact on jobsites. According to research conducted by LinkedIn, the world's largest professional business network on the internet, numerous incidents of racism have been reported in 2020 on construction sites over a six-month period.

Derogatory, racist-based, and inappropriate rhetoric that encourages prejudice and biases for or against an individual can have extremely hurtful implications. Stereotypical comments such as "Don't you only eat rice?" or "Let her figure it out; she's supposed to be great at math," or "Don't worry about her; she's submissive and won't care what we decide," are all forms of denigrating someone.

As a reminder, this is an industry that continues to suffer from skilled labor and professional workforce shortages; such negative environments will only keep potential employees away. These comments can leave people of color and minorities feeling demeaned, belittled, and pushed away. In addition, with so many competing industries, the construction industry is also challenged and faced with attracting Gen. Y and Z: more reason for those of us in the construction industry to focus our efforts on employee retention and inclusivity goals.

Additionally, it is important to acknowledge how stereotypes can lead to increased turnover, absenteeism, low morale, resentment, and unproductive relationships and performance.

In the construction industry, safety is a critical issue on and off a construction site, and professional consulting firms and general contractors often require all members of the team to protect one another because safety is everyone's responsibility. This is the culture and expectation the industry embraces, and it is a culture that needs to be extended into welcoming an inclusive and diverse workforce. The safety philosophy is, if you see something (an unsafe environment) you are empowered and encouraged to say something. Inclusivity and diversity should carry the same amount of significance. As companies brag about their safety record and low number of incidents, I'd like to see them also brag about the diversity in their workforce and the number of women in leadership roles.

In 2020, numerous articles have documented and revealed how Asian workers have not been immune to negative attacks. In fact, there has been a rise in incidents directed towards Chinese or Asian ethnicities because of COVID-19. CBS News White House correspondent Weijia Jiang reports on the growing number of racist attacks many Asian Americans have had to face. Her report tells us that for the period from March to June 2020, over 2,120 hate incidents or crimes were reported by Asian Americans; this according to the Asian Pacific Policy and Planning Council and Chinese for Affirmative Action. This is a staggering 845% increase compared to all the reported cases in 2017, 2018, and 2019 combined. This increase is alarming and has been exacerbated by the use of words such as "Kung Flu" or the "Chinese/China virus." In fact, as I complete the preparation of this book in anticipation of its imminent publication, there are news reports circulating about the possibly racially-motivated killings of several Asians in the Atlanta area.

This pandemic has clearly sparked an awakening and a new wave of "in-your-face racism." This is the yin, now let's focus on the yang.

I sincerely hope these unwarranted attacks end as the country begins to heal and shift its focus towards recovery. As we officially embark on the third and fourth phase of the largest mass-vaccination effort in American history, I am also hopeful that under the new and more diverse administration we will be able to focus on how we can all promote an agenda that will accelerate the transformation of a sustainable and equitable economy. After a tough 2020, Asian Americans are hoping to see a more *United* States of America in 2021. In order to accomplish this, we must remain present and proactive in the communities in which we live and in the jobs that we do.

Thankfully, segments of the construction industry have already begun to take steps to ensure a more diverse and welcoming work environment. In particular, large professional services firms and general contractors have committed to the Justice, Equity, Diversity and Inclusion (J.E.D.I.) Initiative. They have human resources talent and leaders in this department to foster and ensure a collaborative environment exists within their companies' culture. Their initiatives include enhancing opportunities for communication and cultivating a sense of belonging for everyone. They are recruiting and conducting outreach by tapping into diverse groups and organizations to make sure everyone has access to the opportunities available. These efforts, however, shouldn't just fall on HR, talent acquisition, or the J.E.D.I. team; they should be a responsibility shared by everyone in the company. By integrating the J.E.D.I. principles they are proactively promoting and enhancing their ability to respect and accept all people.

Another key element of the benefits of implementing the J.E.D.I. Initiative is the importance of employee satisfaction. We probably all know by now that this is directly linked to customer satisfaction and for that reason alone, we should wholeheartedly and enthusiastically embrace these principles into the company culture. Who wants to be part of this J.E.D.I. task force? Sign me up!

And of course, none of this is possible without having respect for oneself and for each other.

Respect is very much a core attribute of the Asian upbringing. You've likely seen examples of this depicted in American movies: from respecting your parents' wishes in *Crazy Rich Asians* to respecting the martial arts in *Karate Kid* ("Wax on! Wax off!") and countless numbers of Bruce Lee and Jackie Chan movies. As a young girl growing up in Asia, respect is probably the first thing we are taught as soon as we are released from our mother's womb. It is such a large part of growing up Chinese that it's almost as important, if not more so, than scoring straight A's in school. In most Asian cultures, respect of our elders is ingrained in us. As Chinese children growing up in Malaysia, we are taught to respect our grandparents, our parents, aunties, and uncles. We even greet our elders by their ranking – "How are you, first aunty, second aunty, or third aunty. Welcome to our home." We literally have to greet them based on their seniority.

As kids, we had to go around to all the family members to greet and acknowledge them and thank them for visiting our home. This show of respect was mandatory for all visitors. We would greet them with our words followed by a submissive and respectful approach in our body language – a gentle nod in acknowledgement of their presence. Then we (kids) would sit quietly in the corner while the elders chitchatted for hours and shared tea and cookies or small local delicacies (kuih). This was just another way of showing our hospitality and respect. Once again, it was our practice to wait patiently, hoping to hear our parents compliment us in front of our relatives and or visitors, "Good girl" or "Good boy" and it would be even more meaningful if the compliment came from the visitors. Score!

Misbehaving when guests were visiting was not an option. Basically, we didn't get to run around and pretend like they were not there.

Another tradition of respect that continues to take place today happens at the dining table.

While dining at a traditional Chinese restaurant, it is common to acknowledge and first serve your grandparents followed by your parents before anyone else gets to dig in. It is a sign of respect for our elders. The traditional dinner usually includes a lazy Susan that sits in the middle of the round table. The lazy Susan is a revolving tabletop that holds all of the different varieties of food. Once we serve our elders, we then invite them to take the first bite; this is also a gesture of being polite. It was our job as kids to show our respect and to allow them to have the first bite before anyone else. The tradition and expectation still prevail today.

One of the many things I love about growing up Chinese in Malaysia is that this tradition continues despite the many generations, and it brings me joy to be able to show respect for my elders when I am home visiting. These dinners are usually a two- to three-hour affair and consist of a delicious and memorable eight- to ten-course meal. When it's all said and done, we struggle to get off our seats and are usually hanging on to our bellies as we waddle our way out of the restaurant.

In addition to respecting our elders, we also place a lot of significance on respecting each other, no matter the age, status, or rank. It is customary to automatically give respect to everyone around us.

I have heard that in other cultures, you have to earn someone's respect before you get it. In my upbringing and culture, we are taught to give everyone respect no matter what, and it's up to every individual to maintain that respect. Whenever I approach a new position in a new company, based on how I was raised, I automatically walk into every situation by giving everyone equal amounts of respect, regardless of their position or title.

I am reminded of this poignant saying attributed to Dave Willis: "Show respect even to people who don't deserve it; not as a reflection of their character, but as a reflection of yours."[10]

Part of the reason so many stereotypes exist is largely due to the lack of understanding and respect for each other. If you are encountering any kind of disrespect in an office environment, I want you to know that it is worth your time getting to know the colleague who is having a hard time with you. You owe it to yourself to make the first move and to create the opportunity for you to get to know each

10   Original source unknown.

other. In addition, taking the first step makes you the bigger and kinder person.

If you have tried this on numerous occasions and this particular individual is still pushing back, continues to be un-collaborative, or continues to be disrespectful, then you may have to elevate it with your supervisor. But I do want to encourage you to try to resolve the issue yourself and to give the working relationship your best shot. Be your authentic self, try to communicate by sharing who you are, and approach this individual with respect and professionalism. Invite them to be an ally or supporter of an initiative at work. Suggest reasons for collaboration. It may be the start of a productive and dynamic partnership. Don't allow a misconception or a stereotype to dictate the success of your professional relationships.

In sales the most successful business developers are the ones who are able to make friends from strangers and then with time and trust are able to convert those relationships into strong and loyal allies. The best business developers are the ones who authentically invest in their client and industry relationships by bringing value even when there isn't an immediate opportunity in sight. If nothing else, the payoff for establishing mutual respect and a deeper connection is a long-lasting relationship built on trust, openness, and appreciation for each other's perspectives. Very rarely have I heard that getting to know someone better has backfired on anyone.

If, however, you are shy and are an introvert, this is the perfect time to turn a yin into a yang. Use this as an opportunity to hone your interpersonal and social skills because how you interact with others will help you grow your career in the future. By doing this and investing in yourself, you are respecting who you are. Ask yourself, what is your elevator speech? If you don't already have one, it's definitely time to develop one. I ask all my interns and mentees this. If someone says, "Tell me something about yourself," how would you respond? What are the three or four key takeaways you want people to know and remember about you? What do you want someone else to learn about you in 30 seconds? And then if you had a minute, what would you add to the 30-second elevator speech? Start thinking about this now; practice makes perfect.

It's important to start practicing now, because you never know when you'll be stuck in an elevator with a potential employer or client. I can't begin to tell you how many times I've met a client unexpectedly while waiting for my car or at the lobby prior to an event. I have often run into someone I've been meaning to connect with and have had to quickly say something about who I am and the company I work for.

If you are new to a company, go out of your way to socialize with your colleagues – every one of them. Even the unfriendly ones. Seek out common areas of interest. "I noticed you are a huge Kobe fan." "I saw the last proposal you worked on and I was immediately impressed by your work." "I understand you are currently fostering three dogs." "Someone told me you are a scratch golfer." All of these icebreakers will create a much friendlier work environment. If you only keep to yourself, people will assume what they want to assume about you. If you only keep to yourself, their assumptions of you will dictate how they ultimately treat you. I've witnessed this for myself, and as an Asian woman there are multiple categories of stereotypes that are immediately placed on us, so communicating is key in the creation of better relationships.

Have you ever noticed that the individuals who are well networked are usually more successful than the quiet ones who stick to themselves and who hardly say anything? The secret is the more we connect and learn about each other, the better we will understand

and respect one another, and this will help strengthen our network. Understanding a person's culture, likes and dislikes, personal journeys, and passion allows us to relate and be more supportive of each other. This is also one of the best ways to demystify any potential stereotypes.

Sharing and speaking up will also allow you to develop your personal brand. Your personal brand is your business card, so use your voice and use your skill sets to show them who you are. Let your personality and performance speak on your behalf. Turn misconceptions and disrespect into opportunities for establishing respectful relationships. By allowing others to get to know you, you have created a window of opportunity for endless possibilities. In life and especially in business, the depth and breadth of your network can profoundly impact your profession.

So much of what I do today as a business developer is about educating our clients. It's about educating everyone in the industry about who we are, the services we offer, and what we do best. But before I am given the opportunity to educate them about the firm, I must first establish a baseline connection with them. A highly successful business developer understands the value of a relationship and it starts with the ability to connect at a personal level. My ability to establish and build relationships has supported my efforts greatly in a professional environment. Use your time wisely and invest in these relationships and watch the benefits unfold.

There will be times when conflict is unavoidable, and some relationships simply don't work. Healthy disagreements and discussions are a great way to come up with great ideas and different perspectives, as long as the conversations are handled respectfully.

However, if someone continues to stereotype and disrespect you, take the time to figure out the cause of the prejudices. Seek to understand first so you can figure out the best way to approach the situation. Know that nothing starts without respect – respect for yourself and your ability to respect others. When in doubt, remember this: the world is changed by your example, and not by your opinion.

**"I've learned that people will forget what you said, people will forget what you did, but people will never forget how you made them feel."– Maya Angelou**

# CHAPTER 10

# I AM A WOMAN; I BRING SOMETHING UNIQUE AND VALUABLE TO EVERY DISCUSSION

We are so fortunate to live in a time where we are able to witness and welcome so many "firsts." This is indeed a very exciting time in history.

Meet Suely Saro, the first Cambodian American elected official in the history of the City of Long Beach, California. Suely, like those of many younger generations who came to America, had a significant role to play in the family. She served as her parents' interpreter and found herself speaking up not just for her parents but for the community in which she lived. It occurred to her that there were people whom government reached and there were also parts of the community that it did not. Because of that she felt a sense of responsibility to ensure that everyone had a voice. Her actions prevented the community from being marginalized or disenfranchised. Did you know the City of Long Beach has the nation's largest concentration of Cambodian American refugees? The city now has its first female Cambodian American council member. What a great way to have this segment of the population represented in government.

Following in Suely Saro's political footsteps is 25-year old Jocelyn Yow. If you have never heard of her, I promise you, you will. Jocelyn made California history in 2020 by becoming the youngest woman of color to serve as mayor in the history of the state. As we have all seen, the world of politics is a very heavily male dominated arena, regardless of where you are in the world. Even in the world's most culturally-progressive nations, women make up a mere fraction of people in authority. But that didn't stop this Malaysian-Vietnamese-American. Jocelyn stayed true to her passion. A daughter of a Chinese Malaysian father and a Vietnamese refugee mother, she was born in San Jose, California. However, Jocelyn moved to Kedah, Malaysia, where she lived for the next 10 years of her life. This move was prompted by her paternal grandfather's cancer diagnosis.

At 16 she moved back to California, eventually settling down in the city of Eastvale, just one hour away from Los Angeles. In 2018, she became the first Malaysian-American to be elected to public office in the U.S., serving in the Eastvale City Council and then moving on to work as a district representative for the California State Senate, as well as an aide in the U.S. House of Representatives. Today, as the mayor of Eastvale, California, she plans to continue advocating for female representation in politics. I am so proud of my Chinese Malaysian "sister" for making her mark and for making history.

Another great example is Kim Ng, the new general manager of the Miami Marlins. She is Major League Baseball's first female and first Asian American (of Chinese and Thai parents) general manager. In an interview with ESPN, Kim mentions that she had been in the conversation regarding the general manager position for more than a decade before finally landing the job with the Miami Marlins, thanks to CEO and part owner, Derek Jeter. Prior to that she had interviewed for other MLB GM jobs more than a half-dozen times since 2005. She interviewed with multiple teams – the Phillies, Mets, Giants, Dodgers, Mariners, and Padres, but none offered her the position until 2020.

For an entire decade, whenever the question "Who will be the first female GM in MLB history?" was asked, her name typically made the top of the list. But because she didn't look the part, she was never given the opportunity to have the position until now.[11] Thanks to her persistence, hard work, and tenacity, she finally shattered the glass ceiling by becoming the first female general manager in a major North American men's professional sport. After 30 years of rising through the ranks, this acknowledgement couldn't be more well deserved. Kim was determined and pressed on by staying focused on her passion and allowing her performance to shine. She never gave up and believed the impossible would someday be possible and it paid off.

The Los Angeles County Board of Supervisors is considered the most powerful local governmental body in the country. For the first time since the board's inception more than 150 years ago, the board and county made history in 2020 by electing an all-woman board.

To put things in perspective, the board oversees the county's $35 billion budget, the largest jail system, and one of the largest public health infrastructures in the country. With over 10 million residents in Los Angeles county, if LA County were to be a country, it would have the 19th largest economy in the world. In addition to being

---

11  Tyler Kepner and James Wagner, "Kim Ng Has Been Ready for Years," *The New York Times*, November 18, 2020, https://www.nytimes.com/2020/11/18/sports/baseball/kim-ng-miami-marlins.html.

an all-woman board, the board now consists of a Hispanic, three Caucasians, and one African American, each of whom comes with an extensive background in public service, politics, and government. As a Los Angeles County resident, I am excited about our future under the leadership of these five capable and inspiring women.

Speaking of inspiring, it would be remiss of me not to mention Vice President Kamala Harris. Vice President Harris makes history as the first woman and woman of color, first Black, and first person of South Asian descent to be elected to the country's second highest position in office. The daughter of an Indian mother and a black Jamaican father, she has risen higher in the country's leadership than any woman has ever done before. During the race, she endured vicious sexist attacks and name-calling, and despite all that, she handled the bullying with grace and pragmatism. She intensified her message on unity and inclusivity. She empowered people to understand that they too can fit in and fight for what they believe in. Regardless of your political beliefs, there's no denying that her election victory is a positive step towards inclusivity in what used to be considered positions for white men only.

Personally, what I admire most about her is her constant reminder of all the men and women who have come before us and who have paved the way for us to accomplish things beyond our wildest imagination. She consistently highlights their sacrifices by honoring our ancestors. Vice President Harris embodies the future of a country that is growing more racially diverse and inclusive.

Finally, even though she is not of immigrant roots, on a daily basis, I have the pleasure of working with someone who is smart, full of ideas, approachable, a trailblazer, and a clear visionary. I get to have the front-row seat at work to see a woman thrive and inspire others in a male dominated industry. Her name is Wendy Cohen. Wendy was recently named President of Kitchell CEM, assuming leadership of one of the largest construction management firms in Sacramento, California. She is also the first female to be named President of one of Kitchell's five operating companies in the company's 70-year history. It's so refreshing to see and hear from a woman in a leadership position, knowing that she is actively building a path to success for all women in the construction industry.

I think it goes without saying that these women are flipping the script by occupying positions traditionally held by men. The normalization of women in any of these positions leaves a long-lasting and impactful impression. What we are witnessing extends far beyond the fact that they are women; what we are seeing is the variety of women and the value each of them brings to their positions. Their representation in key decision-making roles gives all of us hope, a fair chance at opportunities, and a level of comfort and encouragement to be bold. As an Asian immigrant woman in America, this is highly encouraging and is a powerful game changer for me.

I am reminded of the saying by Theodore Roosevelt: "Nothing worth having comes easy."

Speaking from experience, I will be the first to admit that the path to success has not been easy for me, and I am sure the women mentioned here have had to navigate a series of stereotypes with very challenging career paths as well, some much more than others. When I arrived in Los Angeles in 1999, I didn't know a single person in this city of 10 million people. I didn't have any friends and I didn't have relatives in the area whom I could visit for a free meal. My parents remained in Malaysia. They had never lived in America; they were on the other side of the world in a completely different time zone and I didn't have an existing network I could tap into or rely on. Again, like a good Chinese daughter, I never burdened my parents with my challenges.

Without cousins or uncles to introduce me to their network of friends, I spent the weekends exploring Los Angeles on my own, figuring out what was where and how I was going to make it in the City of Angels. Simply said, I never had a built-in support system in America. There was nowhere to hide or seek refuge. I was on my own to figure out the path I was going to take.

I did, however, arrive in LA to a job, and thankfully I was able to connect and meet some amazing people through work. Today, I am proud to say I have a solid group of friends who are there for me and who would show up if my car broke down, literally. In fact, the last time my car broke down was after a hike with my dog in the summer of 2019. I had two friends show up to help me and one of them was a client. I am grateful for the relationships that have come into my life and have contributed in a meaningful way, no matter how small. Today, I have client relationships at just about every major public agency in Southern California. These relationships are built on years of communication, trust, credibility, and value, and it goes both ways. These are individuals I can go to for advice, for input, and for updates on just about anything. We discuss the economy, their plans for the future, current concerns, budget issues, and how they are navigating the new normal. The conversations often include their kids' activities, anniversaries, golf games, vacations, potential retirement plans, and pets.

So how was I able to chart my course and develop the circle of friends around me? Being independent at a young age has certainly helped me find my way in America. My independence and self-awareness allowed me to navigate many uncomfortable and precarious situations. Knowing when to say something and when to hold back has helped me stay clear of many negative situations and negative people. Two of the earliest lessons I learned from my parents and my dad especially, are to be nice to others and not to judge a book by its cover. Stereotyping and acting on it in a derogatory and unpleasant way is the polar opposite of these teachings.

A key disadvantage to stereotyping is that it makes us ignore differences between individuals and it automatically diminishes their value. Therefore, what we think about someone and how we judge them can likely be a recipe for disaster from day one, especially when starting out in a new relationship. Despite my early independence and self-awareness, I do wish I had been more aware of how to handle certain relationships in my 20's and 30's. Life has a funny way of continuously throwing us curve balls and more often than not, it comes in the way of relationships. The interruptions and life lessons that happens however, gives us the opportunity to evolve and grow as long as we embrace the "yin" life throws at us, and we leverage the "yang." As I continued to mature and evolve, I relied on my instincts and, of course, the core values my parents raised me on, which were to always be respectful and helpful.

If you are walking into work every day and having to deal with a bully or someone who continues to throw negative vibes your way, I hope you use it as an opportunity to find yourself and to grow from it. Don't let this be a missed opportunity. This is an appropriate time to reflect and gather aspects of encouragement and guidance for your personal journey. I want to encourage you to challenge yourself, to not only exceed your own expectations, but also those of the people around you. Let the naysayers judge and say what they want about you, but use it as an opportunity to shine. Surprise them with your intelligence, tenacity, and kindness, and rise to discover your best self. Invite and allow them to see the real you and your contributions to the team.

With most immigrants I know, as much as it seems to be in our DNA to work hard, it is also in our DNA to not ask for any favors.

All we want is to have equal opportunity, to be recognized, and for someone to say thank you. The bigger question is, in a world seemingly obsessed with wanting to embrace diversity but unsure about how best to do so, what are our next steps? How can we help make the world a better place?

Certainly, starting with a united and collective vision helps.

Legendary author and inspirational speaker Jim Rohn reportedly said, "You are the average of the five people you spend the most time with."[12]

What does this mean to us? What this communication expert is trying to teach us is when it comes to relationships, we are greatly influenced — whether we like it or not — by those closest to us, the people with whom we spend the most time. The people we call our circle of friends directly affect our way of thinking, our self-esteem, and ultimately our decisions and how we perceive others. Of course, everyone is their own person, but research has shown that we're more affected by our environment than we may think.

Based on this knowledge I want to encourage you to focus on YOU and your network.

Managing yourself and how you spend your time is the most important investment you will ever make for yourself. It will improve the opportunity to maximize your potential. Your time should be spent on learning something new and meeting or getting to know someone new every day. In business development there is a saying I wholeheartedly believe in and an entire book based on this theory. It is titled *Never Eat Alone*, and it was written by Keith Ferrazzi. It reminds us that we should take advantage of the time we have on a daily basis to get to know someone else or to get to know someone

---

12   Aimee Goth, "You're The Average Of The Five People You Spend The Most Time With," *Business Insider* (July 24, 2012), https://www.businessinsider.com/jim-rohn-youre-the-average-of-the-five-people-you-spend-the-most-time-with-2012-7.

better. The book emphasizes why we should all invest in the development of identifying fulfilling and mutually beneficial relationships, as well as why building your network is a necessity for success.

We've all heard the saying, "It's not what you know, it's who you know." This theory of "never eat alone" rings true with this saying, especially in business. As I look around me and study the circle of friends in my life today, I see a mixture of ethnicities: Black, White, Asian, Persian, Jewish, and many other mixed races. They range in age groups, statuses, jobs, upbringing, experiences, and cultures. As an example, I don't only hang around other Asians. My circle of friends supports and adds to the overall value I bring to everyone else around me. Their varied experiences, influences, and backgrounds complement who I am as I continue to evolve into a better person.

You should expect your friendships and your network to inevitably evolve over time. Sometimes there are friends who fall off the list so you can make room for new connections. There will be ebbs and flows; it's part of the yin and the yang. When one door closes another one opens, it's just part of life.

Personally, I seek friendships that help me increase my intellectual, spiritual, and emotional capacity – friends who ask questions and also friends who are able to provide educated responses to issues I am unfamiliar with. I welcome learning and hearing someone else's opinion on things so I can grow and better understand how and why certain decisions are made. I make no room for anyone with a selfish agenda or a negative attitude.

According to Jim Rohn, ultimately your value is dependent on the people with whom you surround yourself. If you are surrounded by people who are consistently positive, you will automatically have a positive outlook on things and that makes you a highly valued individual. When you are able to see things more clearly, are confident about your decisions, and go out of your way to support others, you are contributing to the overall health and well-being of the people around you and this lends itself to making the world a better place. It is a domino effect, a chain reaction of nothing but good things.

In addition to identifying a strong core group of friends, I believe it is just as important to know your business. Be an expert at your job, whatever that may be. Be so good that if you ever left your position, the team would immediately feel your absence. This is what I strive to accomplish every day.

In the construction industry, the market is beyond saturated with competition and I am seeing more and more companies claiming they can do everything we can. To set ourselves apart we have to ask ourselves the tough questions: How are we protecting our client's best interest better than any other firm? How are we addressing their concerns? What value does our team bring to a project? This is where our ability to speak to the market conditions, supply chain concerns, cost escalation, speed to market capabilities, and risk mitigation strategies, in addition to having a proven team and process, sets us apart.

I'd like to think we are different because of how we communicate our customized approach and solutions, which also then highlights our ability to show an intimate understanding of the client's needs. Our capacity to move things forward, eliminate disputes, and enhance the team's performance is all critical to winning a contract. Of course, none of this really matters if a collaborative environment is non-existent.

Did you know women typically have the edge in collaborative environments because of our listening skills, inclusive body language, and our ability to empathize? These combined factors make us highly valued communicators and leaders. Regardless of the industry you represent, business development and in any sales related position, your knowledge and how well you communicate with the people around you is a determining factor of how others will treat you. In addition, the breadth and depth of your network adds to your overall value. In summary, your ability to intelligently speak to your business is your credibility. The combination of being a skillful communicator is what makes you unique and will get you the attention of your peers and the industry and more importantly, potential new clients.

What I have witnessed this year is encouraging. So many women leaders have had to step up to be braver than usual. We've had to confront harsh realities as we live in these unprecedented times. The year 2020 in particular has highlighted the existing inequalities in our governments and our workplaces and how minorities and women of color are disproportionately represented in all segments. These are the continued challenges we will face in the years ahead. To overcome them, we must lead authentically, acknowledging what we know and what we don't know. We must be intentional about inclusion, recognizing the unique strengths that each person brings, if we intend to achieve our collective goals. We must be purposeful in our commitment to creating and empowering other leaders, especially those who are still underrepresented today. As women, if we continue building on this momentum, we will be able to guide and lead the organizations and the communities where we live towards prosperity from a collective purpose. When that happens, we will all discover more of our value and our ability to make the world a better place.

Strive to be your best authentic self. Harness your inner potential so that others can recognize and appreciate your value.

**"I gravitate towards roles where women find strength in very difficult, uncompromising situations but maintain clarity in mind, discipline at heart, and a certain strength in spirit." — Michelle Yeoh**

# Chapter 11

# Every Setback Is an Opportunity for a Memorable Comeback

In Chapters 1, 2, and 3 you read about how my mother was a key influencer in my life starting at the tender age of six when she unknowingly shaped who I was going to be. Little did she know that by ensuring I had the reading and writing skills necessary, I would go off to college to major in broadcast journalism and would eventually use those skills to become a successful business developer and now an author.

When I look back at all the characteristics that make me who I am today, I am without a doubt an even split of my mother and my father. My father is what most people would consider the typical Chinese man: he is the silent type. However, he wasn't much of a disciplinarian; he left that to my mom. I remember him telling me that he didn't enjoy being the disciplinarian because when he was growing up his father disciplined with a heavy hand and as children, they were all extremely scared of their dad. He didn't want us to feel the same way.

My dad taught me how to swim and how to read a clock and introduced me to sushi and sashimi at a very young age. He is also an extremely staunch Christian man and lives by the teachings of the Bible. He is the kind of man you could go to for help and Dad would be ever ready to volunteer or share anything he had, even when he didn't have much to offer. He would consistently give of himself – something that did not bode well with Mom, especially when Dad was being too financially generous. To begin with, we didn't have much to give at all, but he was just that kind of person. He lived up to the virtues of a good Christian man.

As a young girl, I remember having the pleasure of my dad's singing. He played the acoustic guitar beautifully to tunes from Elvis, the Everly Brothers, Cliff Richard, and Donnie and Marie Osmond. Music brought him joy and I now know why he sang so often.

I'd like to dedicate this chapter to my dad because as a Chinese man, he too faced multiple stereotypes that affected him in his career. As a child I remember my dad waking up every morning at 5:00 am so he could leave for work ahead of traffic. He was out of the house by 6:00 am to head into Kuala Lumpur (city), which was a good 60- to 90-minute drive away. He worked for a leading international shipping company in Southeast Asia. Its principal business comprised of owning and operating offshore floating solutions, providing integrated marine services, port management, and all shipping related activities. Dad dedicated 19 years of his life to his job at this company and slowly worked his way up through the ranks.

He started as an office clerk in 1970 and after 19 years he resigned as a chartering manager. When he started, he didn't know much about the business, but by the time he left he was managing a huge amount of cargo. As chartering manager, he played an integral role in the day-to-day business operations. Dad was mainly responsible for two commodities: palm oil and caustic soda. He was expected to source the optimal shipping solution for the cargo, maximizing potential earnings in the most cost-effective manner.

I remember how stressful this job was for him. I remember Dad returning from work and sitting silently in front of the TV for hours before grabbing his guitar. He was decompressing. For the most part, he never talked about the stresses of the job. I believe singing was his way of dealing with the stress and I always happened to come into the room when the strumming began so I could sing along with him.

He persevered through the years because by all accounts it was a decent paying job, and it was an honest way to continue providing for the family. His trajectory stemmed from hard work, commitment, and the willingness to do whatever it took to grow within the company. Unfortunately for him, despite his work ethic and continued dedication, Dad was passed up for several promotions. He never complained publicly about it, but I remember overhearing a conversation he had with Mom about the first time it happened and how disappointed he was that the position was given to someone with far less experience and knowledge about the shipping industry.

At first, all I could gather was that the process was not a fair one, and it wasn't about Dad's performance or his tenure. I later learned Dad was not given the promotion because of the color of his skin; the promotion was given to someone else 10 years younger than he was and with limited shipping container experience.

A couple of years after the first incident, Dad thought he should try again, so with Mom's encouragement, he put in an application for a better position with more responsibility. He was trying to work his way up the corporate ladder. Unfortunately, he was passed up for the position the second time around, not because he couldn't do the job, but again simply because he wasn't of the right ethnicity. We know these decisions were made because on both occasions the promotion was given to a much less skilled and proficient candidate who fell under the right demographic and who had the political relationships to influence the selection.

I remember the difficult conversations he had with Mom, both expressing their disappointment but also both realizing the realities they were faced with. Even as a young girl — I believe I was around 10 or 12 years old then — I could feel the disappointment, anger, and sadness in the air. It was palpable.

What I learned from this is that life is unfair, and nothing is guaranteed. Sometimes no matter how hard we work and how well we perform, other factors outside of our control prevent us from getting the promotion and recognition we deserve. I wish things had been different for my dad because I saw the heavy toll the stress had on him and how much he endured having to face that reality every day. For the majority of his time, he was reporting to someone far less qualified.

I am sure for some of you, this scenario is not uncommon. This sort of discrimination is a very real thing and unfortunately, it continues to happen today. After almost 20 years at the company and after several missed promotions, Dad finally decided to leave for a different opportunity where he became general manager of a private shipping company. After six years as general manager, he happily retired from the position he worked his whole life to get.

This happened to my father in the '70s and '80s and sad to say even in 2020 Asian men continue to be overlooked because of the color of their skin. This kind of adversity is unlike any other. In the fall of 2020 before we went into our second phase of a full COVID lockdown, I had the opportunity to have lunch with a friend from the industry who is also Asian. It was a gorgeous sunny day in Los Angeles, and we found a table right outside of the Korean restaurant. Like me, this individual had almost 20 years of construction industry experience and had worked for large international firms as well as smaller mid-sized construction management firms. He was extremely successful in his own right.

We had a very open and honest conversation about being Asian in America and how COVID-19 revealed a series of reactions towards Asians. I shared with him some of my experiences and he did the same with me. We discussed the different types of stereotypes Asian men face. He willingly admitted that he had to overcome many obstacles. He always had to prove himself by out-performing everyone else on the team. He had to do this to be considered a valuable team member and had to deliver over and over again to keep his position and to have a seat at the table. But no matter how many contracts he would lead and win, he was never given the opportunity to have the leadership position. He was always the deputy, but never the top guy calling the shots. He would often carry the bulk of the workload, strategically supporting key decisions to guide the team towards contract awards, and yet he was never thought of as the lead.

He said being Asian definitely stifled his trajectory and that for some reason he was never taken as seriously as he would have liked, but his work ethic never wavered. Like me, he valued the sacrifices his parents made for him and ploughed through school and the adversities he faced especially in a professional setting. Despite being born and raised in America, he continued to be, in his words, "glossed over" when it came to leadership positions. So much so, that he decided that second place just wasn't good enough anymore. In recent years, he started his own company. Today his success is no longer dictated by someone else. Today he is happily calling the shots and his company has grown rapidly in a short amount of time. What he did was turn a yin into a yang. His setback became his memorable comeback!

Meet Eric Yuan, one of the richest people in America. Eric is the son of geology engineers. He was born and raised in Tai'an, Shandong Province, China. Inspired by Bill Gates, who spoke in Japan in 1995, he moved to Silicon Valley in 1997 to join the excitement and growth of the tech industry boom. Like many immigrants he came to America hardly speaking any English. Talk about tenacity! He applied nine times before being granted a visa to the United States. I would have probably given up after the fifth attempt. In 2007, he finally became a naturalized American citizen.

Eric's entrepreneurial spirit combined with his determination proved fruitful in America. He got the idea for his creation while trying to find a way to connect with his long-distance girlfriend. At that time, he couldn't convince any investors to back his new venture, but that didn't discourage him. Instead, he did what most entrepreneurs starting out would do – he borrowed money from friends and family to launch what millions of Americans are using today: a video communication platform known as Zoom.

He shares that when his girlfriend saw the countless rejections from tech investors, she too questioned his obsession. His response was "But if I don't try it, I'll regret it." Today, Eric is one of only a handful of Chinese Americans to lead a major Silicon Valley company. The company is now worth $35 billion and employs almost 3,000 people. Curious as to what Eric's motto is? "Hard work and stay humble."

As the founder and CEO of Zoom, he has made over $12 billion since March 2020 and now ranks among the 400 richest people in America.

Then there's Stephen Tang, another epitome of a Chinese immigrant story in America. Stephen is the President and CEO of OraSure Technologies, a medical testing company that is currently developing new COVID-19 testing solutions. The company he leads develops, manufactures, and markets medical devices and diagnostic products. OraSure is on the frontlines of the battles against HIV, Ebola, and now, COVID-19. Their OMNIgene®·ORAL saliva collection and stabilization device, developed by wholly-owned subsidiary DNA Genotek, is utilized in molecular tests for COVID-19 and was recently named one of Time's Best Inventions of 2020. The company is also developing an oral fluid antibody test and a rapid antigen self-test for COVID-19. Dr. Stephen Tang is a son of immigrants. His parents, who emigrated from China, were both scientists.

For Dr. Tang, the issues around racial inequities are personal. As the son of immigrants growing up in Delaware in the 1960s, he faced racism growing up; he and his brother were the only Asian kids in the neighborhood. In a recent article in which he was interviewed, he shared that his personal encounters gave him a window into the injustices that immigrants face. As he grappled with his own experiences, he also made a conscientious choice to share his personal journey with his employees. Despite his negative experiences Dr. Tang turned many yins into yangs.

Today, his contributions are truly exemplary. His leadership is impacting not only Americans, but also the entire health care community throughout the world in a meaningful way. He believes his life's work is to belong, lead, and elevate others in communities near and far.

Dr. Tang also reminds us that the pathway of an entrepreneur and the pathway of an immigrant are very similar. How so? They both require entering worlds they don't really understand and he saw that with his parents in the pursuit of the "American Dream."

I can certainly relate to knowing about entering a new world because I literally did that as a young girl. When I first arrived in America, I had no idea how I was going to be self-sufficient and successful. But what I did do was work really, really hard and I spent a whole lot of time observing others in leadership roles. How they spoke to people, how they managed their teams, and how carefully important decisions were made. In fact, I think I spent all of my 20's just listening, observing, and taking mental notes on how successful people interacted with public officials, the C-suite, and their team members. I watched closely how my bosses led meetings, how agendas were developed and why some worked, and some didn't.

It was that kind of new learning environment coupled with hard work that allowed me to begin my journey towards discovering my career and the American Dream.

For Dr. Tang, it was that perseverance and determination he and his family embraced that didn't allow them to be deterred.

Dr. Tang's story is a reminder that we should not allow any form of stereotype or bullying to define our future. With the right mindset and initiative and an incredible amount of hard work, we are able to accomplish great things. What's so remarkable about his story is while he has achieved great success far beyond his parents' imagination, he has continued to pay it forward in more ways than one. Watching his parents' struggles and having to live through his own hasn't prevented him from wanting to serve communities near and far.

Today, his life's work is to lead his team of scientists, and they are revolutionizing the way COVID tests are being conducted. Their work is helping to save millions of lives.

What I find admirable about my dad's journey and these stories is their unbreakable spirit.

When I was conducting the necessary research for this book, I was thrilled to find a famous international writer and filmmaker who shared the same philosophy as it pertains to dealing with stereotypes. She too approached and leveraged stereotypes the way I did. Her name is Ava DuVernay and, she is best known as the writer and filmmaker of *Selma*, the first film directed by an African American woman to be nominated for a Best Picture Oscar.

She shares that as she moved into positions of power, she found that men questioned her position, and would intentionally make life less than easy. She admits that, from her experience, women who push the envelope often find themselves facing a myriad of new challenges. She adds that as women we can take on these stereotypes and rise to the occasion to meet and exceed expectations by making a simple shift in how we approach the work we do.

I, for one, will be the first to admit that I have been able to overcome challenges that have come my way by staying focused on the end game and by holding true to my ability to deliver.

There are no shortcuts; sometimes you just have to take the time to do the hard work. As my mom would say, "Sometimes you just have to take the bull by the horns and then hope for the best."

I come across a lot of women in their 20's who are eager to climb the corporate ladder and want to contribute in a meaningful way but are unsure how to begin the process and how to earn their seat at the table. While I appreciate their enthusiasm to be taken seriously and to have the fancy titles of Directors and Vice Presidents, I remind them, at the end of the day knowledge is power and the more knowledge you acquire, the more opportunities will present themselves. I also go on to let them know that the knowledge acquired means nothing if they are unable to share what they know in a collaborative manner, and this is where how well one communicates comes into play.

Inspiring women like DuVernay have figured out a way to master every aspect of their craft and they do all this by staying focused, further allowing them to defy the odds. They don't succumb to the pressures and stereotypical roles imposed by society on women, especially women of color. DuVernay has accepted every challenge and excelled by proving the critics wrong. Her philosophy encourages us to look beyond the stereotypes and towards our own potential. I love that!

Successful women like DuVernay are limitless because they are thriving and are imagining a future that has not yet arrived.

As a business developer, I understand that my success is wholly dependent on an anticipated outcome. Every single activity on my calendar has a sole purpose of influencing a decision in the future. As I meet new business developers coming into the industry, my most common recommendation is for them to master the art of establishing a relationship and, following that, truly learn how to maintain a relationship by being a valuable conversationalist. That to me is the most important aspect of any sales position. Why is this important? It is important because the best relationships are the ones that continue to add value and are eventually reciprocal.

In the world of business, whether you are sharing something new with your client, something he/she wasn't aware of, what's happening within the industry, or what RFP's were just released that affect the overall market, these are all pieces of information that add value. You want your client to walk away from a conversation with you thinking, "I am so glad we caught up."

Your ability to bring value regardless of the circumstance will make you a highly desirable team member with unlimited possibilities.

Trailblazers like DuVernay embolden us by unveiling the power in sharing our struggles, and stories like hers keep me motivated and inspired.

There are many common threads from all the stories I've shared with you in this chapter. Each of them turned the yin into a yang. They were all self-motivated, and what's obvious is some of the most amazing and impactful ideas and situations haven't come easy and never start out being comfortable. If we want to be successful, we must get comfortable by allowing ourselves to first be uncomfortable. Sometimes that means stepping into the unknown.

Do yourself a favor: stop second guessing your potential. Dive into the unknown and use every learning opportunity as leverage to re-emerge better, stronger, and smarter.

**"I hate to point out the obvious, but here's this tiny bird that's been trying to get through a huge bulletproof glass wall. A totally impossible situation. You tell me it's been here every day pecking away persistently for ten minutes. Well, today the glass wall came down." — Kevin Kwan**

# CHAPTER 12

# SELF-MOTIVATION IS NOT ONLY A BEAUTIFUL THING; IT'S ALSO SEXY

What is self-motivation? Most definitions consider how you can find the ability to do what needs to be done without influence from other people or situations. I am often asked this question: "How are you so self-motivated?" and the answer for me is easy. My reason for being self-motivated is not tucked away in one moment or one tragic experience. It's found in countless years of watching my parents' sacrifices, seeing what they had to do to put the needs and education of me and my siblings before anything else. It's knowing how they ensured we had everything we needed to be successful as adults. All I have to do is reflect on my upbringing and how much my parents had to give up, for me to feel a sudden burst of motivation. Honestly, I am still amazed today by how they raised us with so little. I witnessed aunties and uncles who worked extremely hard and that was the culture in the Lee (father's) and Ong (mother's) families. When you grow up surrounded by so much sacrifice, you are automatically that much more grateful for everything you have and the combination of both makes me and I am sure most immigrants jump out of bed every morning.

In today's environment, we are faced with complex challenges and changing expectations from society and at work. These demands require different kinds of strategies and approaches. Hard work alone isn't sufficient. This means augmenting necessary hard and soft skills and technical expertise by working towards a deeper level of empathy, awareness, creativity, authenticity, purpose, and most of all motivation.

Being self-motivated also means the ball is in your court and what you want to do with it is entirely up to you. We don't necessarily have to defy or conform. To be self-motivated, we can seek to find the yin and the yang, and the balance in all situations while remaining motivated. Now why is self-motivation so important? It is important because it helps you navigate difficult situations; it gives you the drive to push forward, no matter what the obstacles, and it supports your ability to keep your eye on the ball.

If you are struggling to stay motivated, I've found that a combination of several tactics can help you maintain your focus so that you can be unstoppable.

Start by managing your mindset. If you continue to doubt yourself, you will inevitably fail at whatever it is you are trying to accomplish. Surround yourself with people who believe in you and are willing to listen and lift you up. Identify a mentor. Mentors play a crucial role in encouraging you and your dreams and are there to catch you when you fall.

Continue learning because knowledge is power. The more you know about an issue or about something about which you are passionate, the better off you will be. The knowledge you acquire will build your self-confidence. Read a great book or start doing some research. No matter what you decide to do, never stop learning and asking questions.

Start making the necessary changes in your life so you can begin to welcome all the great things that are about to come your way. This could be as simple as rearranging the furniture in your apartment, getting rid of the old so you can make room for the new. My mom would recommend you use Feng Shui to reevaluate the flow in your house. If something doesn't feel right or is getting in the way, move it. Oprah says if you haven't worn it in over two years, get rid of it. Anything that is dragging you down and is not adding value to your life can be dropped off at the Salvation Army or Goodwill. That includes unproductive relationships.

Seek out new experiences, personally and professionally. Work at keeping an open mind, allow yourself to try new things. Look at how other industries are approaching the new normal. Stepping out of your comfort zone or area of expertise triggers many rewarding lessons and insights on a professional and personal level. It can provide many lessons for changing the way we look at a myriad of things. When we seek out new experiences, we are inviting the opportunity to develop new ideas for how we can better approach things.

Know yourself as well as you know your craft. Understand your limitations, so you know when to ask for help. Be sensitive to how much you are managing, so you are acutely aware of what you are willing to do and take on. Know where you bring the best value to the team; knowing this will also help you identify areas of growth. Excel where you can, look forward, and stay engaged. Today's construction landscape is extremely difficult to navigate with its continually changing variables, including project delays and unexpected work stoppages, evolving project requirements, keeping up with scope changes, and satisfying code requirements. Then there's budget, schedule, and funding concerns. Where's the money coming from and when will it get here?

Every aspect of the construction industry is as unpredictable as it is dynamic and exciting. Nothing is certain and the rules of the game change frequently while pressures mount and competitors are chomping at our contract and our people. With all this dynamic tension, as industry professionals we must take a hard look at how we manage our time and our contribution. Now more than ever, we must be clear about our roles, responsibilities, and expectations. Being cognizant of this will help you manage your time and your relationships better and will help you stay motivated.

The goal is to help you stay motivated by maximizing the return on your day-to-day efforts. In addition to knowing my craft, as a business developer, one of the reasons I stay so engaged with the news locally and internationally is that I want to be able to have well rounded conversations with my clients. I want to be able to participate in discussions that impact not only the construction industry but also the community and elsewhere. Having the ability to speak about things happening near and far adds to my value and credibility and allows me to chime in on a conversation. I never want to be in the dark about what's happening in the world and in the industry, especially in front of my clients.

Your overall health and well-being are also reasons to stay motivated.

Maintain a healthy lifestyle so you are sharing your best self and check in on yourself as much as you are checking in on your team. It's OK to ask yourself, how are you doing today? If your response is less than favorable, then re-evaluate what is happening and take the time to resolve it. You can't motivate others on your team if you are not self-motivated.

"Knowing others is wisdom, knowing yourself is enlightenment." – Lao Tzu. Ancient Chinese Philosopher and Writer, Founder of Taoism.

All of these subtle but important steps will help empower you through your challenges. And when you are ready, you will be able to move more confidently into male dominated and unchartered areas. Not only that, you will be excited about speaking up on things about which you are knowledgeable and passionate. With the right mindset, sufficient knowledge, confidence, and nothing holding you back, you will feel the sudden surge in your ability to spring forward. Start cultivating the habit of being unstoppable.

If you are currently in a leadership role, take advantage of your position by channeling the diversity of ideas around you to unlock the possibilities. Embrace and develop a fresh mindset to keep yourself open to new ideas. As humans we are not meant to operate in isolation, so a holistic and inclusive approach is going to be more purposeful and will benefit a greater number of people. In addition, always plan for the future and prepare to react to the unexpected, even if that includes responding to inappropriate or discriminating comments.

Julie Owen is the Deputy Executive Officer of the Program Controls Division of Los Angeles County Metropolitan Transportation Authority (LACMTA). This agency serves as transportation planner and coordinator, designer, builder, and operator of one of the country's largest, most populous counties. It provides public transportation to more than 9.6 million people.

Julie is part of a leadership team committed to providing a world-class transportation system that enhances the quality of life for everyone who lives, works, and plays within Los Angeles County. She is motivated today, more than ever, because of the changes she is experiencing in the construction industry. She recalls joining the agency 12 years ago as one of the only females on the technical team. Since then and thanks to a progressive CEO at the helm, the number of women working for this agency has significantly increased. Today Julie is excited to have an army of women in key leadership roles driving some of the largest infrastructure projects in the country and that, for her, is extremely motivating.

Julie is currently in charge of over $28 billion in infrastructure projects and is simultaneously supporting over 48 on-going projects. She is excited about the future as she continues to tap into the pool of women at LA Metro for their expertise. Julie is also setting an example for the next generation of women to imagine themselves in leadership positions and to reach their full potential. She is one of those women who walks the talk and encourages everyone to join her on the journey.

Julie's journey is part of a larger mission – she is paving the way for other women in a male dominated industry. We must capitalize on this momentum and ensure that every year from here on out is a year for real, positive change, a renewed spirit in support of inclusivity and diversity, and an opportunity to accomplish more. The momentum for all women and all women of color has been brewing and with Vice President Kamala Harris at the helm, we have been given greater purpose. We too can be a "Kamala" at the local level and in our own unique way.

While we have come a long way as women and women of color, we still have a lot to accomplish and our work cut out for us. If you are ever feeling unmotivated, just think about all the women who fought so hard for us to have a voice and an opportunity to be contributors to society. We must not allow their sacrifices to go to waste.

To make substantial progress, however, we must be transparent and proactive and hold ourselves accountable as we encourage industry- and community-wide participation. While we have progressed in our advancement of women, as more females take on leadership positions, especially amongst minorities, we must not allow ourselves to rest on our laurels. We must continue to raise the bar by investing in social equity programs and initiatives that advance inclusion goals. We must focus our efforts on retaining women and under-represented minorities in senior positions. These efforts will require leadership, persistence, investment, and new ways of collaboration, as well as the all for one, one for all mindset.

In a March 15th, 2021 article Bessie Liu of The Org, an organization focused on making companies more transparent in its business practices, shares staggering statistics on the realities Asian women in corporate America face today. "Despite Asian Americans making up almost 12% of the professional workforce whilst being only 5.6% of the U.S. population, studies show that they are the least likely racial group to be promoted to executive positions."[13]

In addition, her report includes an Ascend study which shows that one in 87 white men in the U.S. holds an executive position. This number drops to one in 123 for white women, and one in 201 Asian men. Asian women are among the least likely to be promoted, with only one in 285 likely to hold an executive position.

If this does not provide food for thought and does not trigger an emotion towards the need for change and unification as minority women, I am not sure what will.

---

13  Bessie Liu, "Shattering Asian American Stereotypes in Corporate America", *The Org*, (March 15, 2021), https://theorg.com/insights/shattering-asian-american-stereotypes-in-corporate-america.

Don't forget, your vibe attracts your tribe, so if you are self-motivated you will also have the ability to motivate others around you and that's an incredibly sexy thing.

**"Like most who are underestimated, I have learned to over-perform." —Stacy Abrams, African American Politician, Author, Lawyer, Voting Rights Activist**

# CHAPTER 13

# THE LACK OF UNDERSTANDING CREATES DIVISION AMONGST US. KINDNESS ALWAYS WINS

I love the color of my skin and I am a proud Chinese Malaysian American. Despite all the stereotypes that have been imposed on me — some good, mostly bad — I know that being kind is the right way to handle and approach any form of negativity.

Kindness is an active choice; it takes heart, active listening, and a genuine commitment to doing something good for someone else. When you snub someone, you are being unkind. When you pass someone up for a promotion because of the color of their skin, that too is considered unkind. When you are intentionally uncollaborative, for whatever reason, you are being unkind. I've had a few people be unkind to me for no reason at all. More than half of them hadn't even given themselves the opportunity to know me and my value and how I could have contributed to their efforts. Women and people of color are still underrepresented in many positions because people have been unkind to them. Just like stereotypes, being unkind can be degrading, hurtful, and humiliating for the recipient.

If you are the recipient of someone being unkind to you, I recommend staying rooted in who you are and harnessing your inner strength to manage the situation. Don't allow someone to ostracize and denigrate you; instead, you must work to peacefully claim your spot. Use your intellect and performance as a means to show your value and allow your contribution to speak for itself. Don't retreat or self-isolate; stay relevant and present and thrive on exceeding expectations and then, of course, kill them with kindness. Use these instances as opportunities for growth and self-discovery.

The struggles we face in life make us unique and strong. They allow us to evaluate our priorities and, in the process, we learn how to say no – no to being glossed over, and no to being ignored. We figure out what's important to us, so we can maximize our productivity. We are given the opportunity to pause and refocus, so we are not distracted by things that prevent us from reaching our goals.

Use the yin to discover the yang. In the film and television industry, Asian Americans talk a lot about the need for representation in Hollywood. The truth is there's room for strides in representation in pretty much every field. Not only do Asian Americans have to contend with the glass ceiling, but we also have to worry about the "bamboo ceiling" – an invisible barrier that systematically keeps Asians out of leadership positions in spite of success in the workplace. I will be the first to admit that I am one of the individuals who have had to work vigorously to demonstrate that the bamboo ceiling does not apply to me. I use everything in my toolbox to allow me to perform at a higher level, to appear unbreakable and impervious.

Thankfully, I am also aware of how to find balance and I've done this by recognizing the good, bad, and indifferent. I am comfortable being the overachiever and being in my own skin. I've never allowed myself to be something I am not.

Let's be honest: stereotypes won't disappear unless people truly understand how harmful they are and how much damage they can cause in and outside of the work environment. This is why I felt compelled to write this book. It's a distressing and unwarranted consciousness that continues to happen and so it is a conversation we must continue to have.

Being stereotyped and experiencing social discrimination are not only depressing; these phenomena also create a domino effect of other emotions. Here are some of the signs to look out for: if you find yourself angry all the time, not only at the discriminator but also at others around you; if you feel withdrawn from your team and feel a lack of belonging; if you experience discomfort every time you show up for work and continuously question your purpose, I want you to know that there is hope. Millions of immigrants who have faced extremely tough working conditions and unimaginable suffering and loss have had to dig deep and stay resilient. They have redirected their energy towards the goal of changing the status quo. They've discovered their ability to bounce back beyond the initial setbacks, fostering further development of their skills, relationships, and environment. They reach out to other people who share their struggles so they can support and motivate each other. They continue to be kind.

Individuals who respond to stereotypes with resilience are likely to tap into their coping mechanisms and in the process, help guide others through similar experiences. They do this with unlimited kindness.

We don't have to let these stereotypes define and bring us down. No matter how other people see and treat you, you know deep down inside who you are and what you are made of. Everyone brings a unique perspective and a set of skills and talents to every situation. Every one of us has a special place in this world and it starts by recognizing each other and by being kind to one another.

As an immigrant I have never asked or expected to be treated differently, I don't expect anyone's sympathy and don't expect to be someone's favorite person on the team. In fact, I would rather not be labeled as someone's "favorite" because I wouldn't want to be in a position only because of the people I know. I would much rather earn my seat at the table than for it to be given to me due to anything other than my merit. My preference is to be seen as an equal and to be welcomed by a team of professionals based on my credibility, intelligence, work ethic, and value. I want to be promoted based on my performance and potential, not based on favoritism and proclivity.

Navigating stereotypes requires a personal strategy and a strong foundational moral compass. Every situation has to be dealt with in its own unique way. I want to encourage you to explore how you can remain resilient in the face of adversity by adopting new ways of approaching challenges and overcoming obstacles within your own professional context. I suspect that as you endure the stereotype, you will discover new insights and skills that will impact your overall performance and will empower you to thrive with more clarity and conviction in the future.

When someone approaches you in a negative way, try turning that relationship into an opportunity to be kinder to them. In my experience, kindness always wins! We all know it takes so much more energy to be mean and nasty to someone than it is to be nice and kind to someone. You know what they say, where there is chaos there's opportunity. And with every opportunity comes the birth of a new strategy and approach.

Speaking of a new approach, being kind also means encouraging yourself to have a seat at the table. I always take the opportunity to say, "Go ahead, conference me in." When you are stereotyped, chances are someone is working against you, which means they go out of their way to not include you on things, in meetings, and in discussions. They don't want you in the room because they don't care about your opinion or your value. The truth is they are probably intimidated by you. Don't allow yourself to be excluded from things. Take an active role by choosing to attend a meeting or a series of meetings. The opportunity to learn from others starts when you allow yourself to be included.

In my observation of the construction industry, in the last 10 years or so I have seen an increase in the number of small, minority, and women-owned firms. This proliferation stems from women who want and know they deserve to be included. They've found a creative way to establish their presence and to have a voice. Most have left jobs with much larger companies and salaries, probably because they were never given the opportunity to have a key leadership position with the firm or they felt they couldn't fully dictate their own success.

The rising participation of women in small businesses may be a result of the need to redefine how women are measured and rewarded. The prevalence of stereotypes is also cause for many women to hit the proverbial "glass ceiling," which prevents women from reaching the upper echelons of management in organizations. Many women, therefore, elect to bypass the barrier that prevents them from becoming senior executive officers to start their own firms and businesses.

The dramatic increase in women-owned businesses is an example of how society is changing the game and how women are redefining what it means to be successful. These women have chosen to not allow themselves to be discouraged. They have created their own environment so they can decide where and when they sit at the table and who they invite to the game.

They've taken the yin and redefined the yang in their favor.

We may not be able to avoid stereotypes completely and immediately, but in the interim what we can do is be kinder to one another and allow ourselves the freedom to be included in conversations. Don't let the stereotype make a mockery out of you; remember being misunderstood is an opportunity for you to communicate and connect at a deeper level.

Always choose kindness over judgement. Be a champion of positive change.

**"I am saddened by how people treat one another and how we are so shut off from one another and how we judge one another, when the truth is, we are all one connected thing. We are all from the same exact molecules." — Ellen DeGeneres, Award-winning Talk Show Host, Actress**

# CHAPTER 14

# LEVERAGING STEREOTYPES WITH A PROVEN BUSINESS DEVELOPMENT APPROACH AND STRATEGY

Much of what I have shared in Chapters 1–13 have been universal recommendations as to how you too can leverage stereotypes to your advantage. I have no doubt that the real-life suggestions shared are applicable regardless of your current position or your current industry. With a clear vision as an individual or as a team and by acknowledging and having these conversations, we can begin to walk the talk towards a more equitable and inclusive environment. Now, let's examine how navigating stereotypes is identical to having a successful business development strategy.

I've been very blessed to have an amazing career and have had the pleasure of working with some of the best individuals and teams in the construction industry. Like any work environment, it's the challenges and difficulties that allow us to grow and discover our strengths and weaknesses. My professional story features a combination of successes and failures with lessons learned along the way and some big highs followed by some really low lows. I've experienced it all.

As a business development professional I've had the opportunity to live through these peaks and valleys and have come to the realization that how I have successfully dealt with stereotypes in many ways is identical to how I have successfully navigated and approached my position in business development. Certain attributes and strategies have proven themselves in support of my evolution.

### #1. Never underestimate the power of relationships.

As a business developer, my success is dependent not only on the client relationships I have had to establish, cultivate, and maintain; just as important are the internal relationships at work. My success is dependent on the trust, collaborative nature, and respect of and with the leadership, operations, and marketing teams, and with the regional executives and market sector leaders/subject matter experts with whom I work.

I've always approached my internal team as if they were my clients, and often ask myself, "How can I be of service to them? How can I make their lives better and the process easier? What is my contribution and value-add to the team?"

When dealing with being stereotyped, the most important thing in mitigating and understanding why it is happening is to try to connect with the individual who is giving you a hard time. As difficult as that sounds, it is important to be the bigger person in the situation. If you don't take the first step, you'll end up spending the bulk of your time avoiding this individual or putting up with them. Neither option is a step towards a positive work environment. So as hard as it is, be the one to take the first step to establish a healthier relationship and to demystify any misconceptions. Ask yourself how you can connect with this individual at a deeper level and how you can better serve them so that they do not continue stereotyping. Help them see who you really are.

### #2. Maintain your integrity, don't sell your soul to the devil.

There are a lot of creative ways to secure a contract; I've always said I will only represent and work for a firm that is willing to do the work – one that is willing to earn a contract based on ethical pre-positioning efforts, technical qualifications, merit, proven experience, resources, and reputation. The truth is, none of these things matter if the firm is not ultimately known for its integrity, how it conducts its business, its day-to-day operations, and how it conducts itself within the industry. Wikipedia defines integrity as the practice of being honest and showing a consistent and uncompromising adherence to strong moral and ethical principles and values.

With integrity you don't allow yourself to waver on your core principles; you don't compromise who you are. In dealing with stereotypes you don't alter who you are to accommodate the other person. With integrity you continue to treat everyone the same way, with kindness, respect, and honesty. People who embrace and practice integrity know how to behave by upholding a moral standard of conduct, both in professional and personal endeavors, especially as it relates to how they conduct themselves at work, in the office, or at a conference. Their work ethic, their communication practices, and how they treat others reflect their integrity. In business development, integrity is the most important part of the puzzle for winning work and for developing successful relationships.

### #3. It takes EQ and IQ to deal with being stereotyped.

I can't say I have always done everything right every single time someone has mistreated or disrespected me, but what I have learned is my ability to handle a situation as professionally as humanly possible while maintaining my composure has always served me well. In business development it certainly pays off to have EQ to manage the highs and the lows. Emotional Quotient (EQ) is widely defined as an individual's ability to sense, understand, and effectively apply the power and acumen of emotions to facilitate higher levels of collaboration and productivity. EQ is often referred to as emotional intelligence. To me, EQ is focused on our ability to identify and manage our emotions and, just as important, our ability to be empathetic to others.

IQ is the Intelligence Quotient and it's a measure of a person's relative intelligence. Subject matter experts, market sector leaders, engineers, and architects who are technical experts in their field are expected to have really high IQ's. To manage being stereotyped, I think you have to be smart enough to know how to react to a situation by assessing the environment, the dynamics of the surroundings, and the people around you so you can appropriately navigate the situation and control how you are going to react to it. But it also takes strong IQ so you can truly assess and grasp the complexity of the moment and know how to apply what is going on and react with the proper information.

Studies show successful leaders and superior performers have well developed EQ and IQ skills. The combination of both high EQ and high IQ makes it possible for those individuals to work well with a wide variety of people and to respond effectively to rapidly changing conditions. The most successful and effective leaders with whom I have had the privilege of working are always self-aware, have social skills, operate with integrity, and really know their role and what is expected of them. When being stereotyped, it is critically important for you to be fully aware of your surroundings, to be able to process what is happening with the information you have and to determine how to react without losing control. If you feel you have more of one ability over another, there's hope! Both EQ and IQ skills can be learned.

**#4. Stay humble.**

Humility is probably the second trait ingrained in most Chinese kids after respect.

I remember being in primary school. By then I was already a competitive swimmer in the local club's swim team. We competed often against other clubs and we trained every morning at 5:00 am before school. I loved competing and loved springing off the starting board as soon as I heard the whistle. I was tiny and usually always the shortest in my age group, but that didn't stop me from kicking harder and moving my arms faster. I hated coming in second place; it just meant that I wasn't kicking hard enough.

By age seven I had already begun accumulating medals. While in school one day, a teacher asked, "Who is a good swimmer?" I immediately raised my hand and noticed that only one other girl had done what I had. I looked around the class and it took me a split second to realize that raising my hand and admitting to being a good swimmer was not the right thing to do. The teacher followed her question by saying, "Have you no shame? You shouldn't be bragging about being good at something." She then added that it was very impolite to be bragging. The memory of that lesson has stuck with me since. In most traditional Asian cultures, we are taught to never brag about our accomplishments, that we should allow others to recognize and acknowledge our successes, and that we should politely downplay our abilities and achievements.

As an adult I have continued on this path of self-deprecation, so maintaining my humility has never been an issue for me. It is officially ingrained in every ounce of my body. Sometimes I even have a hard time taking compliments from others, but I will say it is great when your peers recognize your contributions and even nicer to receive credit from your superiors. Most of the time, I am just so grateful when someone says thank you.

Humility is such an important trait in business and in your personal life because being humble allows us to have a realistic and accurate view of ourselves. It also keeps us grounded so we can freely acknowledge our mistakes and limitations. It allows us to be open to other viewpoints and ideas and keeps our accomplishments in perspective. It shifts the focus from making it all about us and more about appreciating the value of all things, including other people. If you are still asking why it's important to stay humble, here's the most blatant answer: no one likes dealing with egomaniacs.

So, what does this have to do with being stereotyped? When you are under attack, it is easy to want to immediately defend yourself or to fight back. Your ability to maintain your humility is, in fact, one of the most powerful attributes you can use to defuse a situation. Humility removes pride from the equation; humility embraces different perspectives and cultivates self-awareness and mindfulness for even the most difficult situations.

**#5. Establish a team of allies – people who believe in you and your ability, people who genuinely care about your success.**

I know from experience, in order to be a successful business developer, you have to have a team of people who believe in your ability and who sincerely care about your overall success. Being stereotyped can be a very precarious situation. Whether you identify with individuals within your company (other Asians as an example) or outside of your company, the advantages to having professional and personal allies — close and trusted friends who are willing to listen and be there for you — is an important piece of your overall well-being. Your opportunity to speak with someone who can relate to what you are going through or to an individual who can sympathize with what happened and continues to encourage you to do the right thing, to maintain your integrity, to stay humble, and to handle things professionally is vital to your sanity and happiness.

In my professional life, I have never seen or met a successful business developer who has worked in isolation and independently of others. Business development is definitely a team sport. It takes a group of people coming together to come up with creative ideas, to identify new clients, and the resources needed to successfully execute a project, and to deliver the project under budget, on schedule, and with the quality intended.

As an example, you can't analyze the competition by yourself. Others may have more current intelligence on the competition of which you may be completely unaware. As a business developer you may have a large Rolodex of contacts but there is always a client with whom you may not have a relationship that someone else in the company may have. And you certainly won't be able to achieve your revenue goals if you aren't working closely with the technical team responsible for executing the work.

If you are being stereotyped and you want to maintain a healthy working environment and a healthy personal life, I encourage you to establish a team of allies – people you trust and friends who will listen, lift you up, and support you through the difficult times. If you don't recognize them immediately, look harder.

**#6. Be the team champion.**

Be your company's biggest cheerleader while being your own champion.

What you want for your company is often what you want for yourself, so when you are cheering others on, you are indirectly cheering yourself on, as well. There is never too much positivity, as long as it comes from a genuine place and the intentions are good and supportive of others.

Have you noticed that in every team sport there is always the team champion? Most team champions are naturally passionate about winning and passionate about watching others accomplish their goals. He or she usually plays the role of team leader, promoting positivity and all good things.

There is a reason so many companies are invested in a community-based company culture – it has obvious benefits. It increases employee engagement and if done right, could also increase a company's industry engagement. With social media today, more and more companies share their employees' individual and team accomplishments. The exposure with social media is limitless, its convenience and accessibility cannot be matched, and everyone and every company needs a team champion to remind us of all the good things we are doing.

What's so great about being a team champion is that you don't need a title to officially be the company's cheerleader. Anyone can do it and be a part of it. You can do it by taking the initiative and spreading the message on behalf of your company, whether it's a ground-breaking ceremony, a newly awarded project, team members who have just completed a marathon, or a charity event with a client. It is important that we continue to celebrate the accomplishments of others because when we do that, we also continue to lift ourselves up. If you are consistently being stereotyped for the color of your skin, your origin, your accent, or your gender, take an active role in being the company's cheerleader and watch the attention change from being stereotyped to being the champion of all people. Change the game by changing the environment. At the end of the day, when we are all lifted, no one gets left behind, especially not you. When we celebrate others, it automatically awakens our hope, motivates our passion, creates a sense of excitement, and gives us reason to continue celebrating and cheering others on. Now go find your pom-poms!

**#7. Live in a constant state of improvement.**

My philosophy with business development is to continue learning from every experience, to continue asking questions and having intelligent, fruitful conversations. I enjoy hearing from a variety of people and gaining different perspectives. It's what makes life interesting and enjoyable. Being stereotyped gives us opportunities to grow, to not just have a better understanding of ourselves and what triggers an emotion, but it also provides an opportunity for us to learn about others – their insecurities, fears, false assumptions, and reactions to things. As we grow and as we learn to understand others, we can also help them to grow and perhaps learn something new about a thing or two.

I remember a day at work when I had to gently tell a colleague that the remarks he had made to another colleague were simply not cool. At first, he was a little defensive, but when I politely explained why it was a hurtful comment, he began to calm down and see how what he said had a negative connotation to it. He then thanked me for being a supportive colleague and took the time to apologize to the person to whom he had made the remark.

I am in no way, shape, or form pretending to take on the role as the ethics police; I am aware that that is not my position. But when you care enough to professionally and gently correct someone for a mistake they unknowingly made, I've found that it pays off in the long run.

I know that when I have said something inappropriate or hurtful, I would prefer to be told right away than for the individual to harbor negative thoughts about me. Sometimes we misspeak; it happens all the time and it takes courage to apologize and to respond to it quickly and genuinely.

In business development, more often than we would like to admit, we spend a whole lot of time pre-positioning for strategic pursuits, a process that could take months and sometimes years. Sometimes, even when you think you have done everything right and better than your competitors; you still end up losing the contract. It's painful but it happens. One of the best ways to understand how we could have done better is to obtain a client debrief. This is a process where you are given the opportunity to better understand your shortcomings or what you and your team could have done better. A debrief or post-mortem can help to uncover flaws in your process and submission and highlight areas of improvement, ultimately ensuring we learn and hopefully aren't making those same mistakes again.

Allowing yourself to be a life-long student in life and at work will only benefit your self-awareness and credibility. No matter what the situation, no matter how seasoned a professional you are and how overqualified you are, I can guarantee you that life will continue to teach you valuable lessons. We are better off embracing lessons life has to offer by having the right mindset so we can continue to grow and learn from every situation. The goal is to come out of every situation smarter, stronger, and better, so choose to live in a constant state of improvement.

#### #8. A little bit of optimism goes a long way.

Depending on the industry you're in, the typical Request for Proposal (RFP) process may involve one or more selection steps before contract award. As a business developer in the construction industry, I spend an average of 50% of my time supporting, leading, or guiding a proposal effort. In business development, a key component of what we do prior to the RFP release, however, is the relationship building and pre-positioning effort that correspond directly to the particular project pursuit needs and expectations.

I remember at the time I started in this field 15 years ago, we would typically compete with five to seven firms for a single contract. Today, however, the number of competitors has tripled and, as I've seen in the last 18 months or so, even quadrupled in some instances. This, of course, significantly impacts the win rate. If you are the kind of person who takes each pursuit personally, is fully invested in the client relationship, and has invested three to five years or more into ensuring your team is best positioned for the job, accepting defeat can be extremely difficult and possibly devastating. I've personally experienced how detrimental the losses and the unexpected results can feel.

As a business developer it is important to have the ability to bounce back after losing a huge contract. We have to allow ourselves to learn from the mistakes and then to quickly pivot and focus on the next pursuit. In order to successfully do this, we have to stay optimistic even when we don't feel like it. We can't allow a major loss to dictate how we move forward or how we approach our next opportunity. As is the case with so many other areas of life, by staying optimistic you open yourself up to allowing good things to come your way. That kind of positivity will also improve your perspective on things and will support how you tackle any new issues or obstacles that may arise. Plus, no one wants to be around someone who exudes negativity.

In dealing with stereotypes, I understand how what someone says can ruin your entire day, or an entire week. You may choose to start avoiding them for months and that can be extremely dejecting. The difference between people who choose to stay positive and those who don't is how they react to negative situations; the ones with the positive outlook find productive and positive ways to cope and respond. They continue to engage in healthy conversations, they surround themselves with positive people, they maintain their sense of humor, and they find ways to manage the stress. I highly recommend yoga, a good hike, a nice long run, or a day on the golf course.

It's been said that positive emotions help speed recovery from negative emotions, so don't underestimate the power of being positive, even if you don't feel like it.

**#9. Keep your eye on the prize.**

You've probably heard the saying "work smarter, not harder." I can't say I agree 100% with that approach. I've always had to work smart *and* work hard. It comes with watching your parents operate the same way their entire lives. It's a hard habit to break, especially when that's all you saw growing up and that's all you know. Like my parents, I've had to work extremely hard in order to have everything I own. Nothing has been given to me. As an immigrant and an Asian woman in a male dominated industry, I've had to earn the respect of others, and to me there was only one way to accomplish that. There was only one clear path to earning that respect, and it involved putting a lot of hours into learning my craft. In business development, one of the most important skill sets is knowing how to stay optimistic and focused; it is critical to keep your eye on the prize by honing in on the end game in every pursuit.

Don't allow unexpected activities or distractions to take over your workday. Keep those distractions in check. Distractions are our number one enemy when it comes to keeping focus. The minutes and hours we spend being distracted can affect our overall performance.

Similarly, hurtful comments and unproductive conversations that stem from a stereotype must be placed into the distraction bin. I know it can be hard to dismiss how someone is negatively treating you, but you have to put things in perspective by prioritizing your thoughts and emotions. When people try to intentionally knock you down, take it as a compliment; it only means they are that much more intimidated by you. Either that or they are just choosing to be ignorant of your real value and or choosing to be mean. Either way, remember the concept of the yin and the yang. Take a negative and make it a positive to find your balance. In those instances, I've always known where and how to spend my time – laser-focused on my performance and my contribution to the team and the overall objective. Don't allow someone else's insecurities to be a distraction from your performance and your positive contribution and attitude. Your job is to stay focused on achieving a positive end result. How can you do this?

You're smart and you've worked hard. The next step is to prepare yourself for success. Prioritize your *priorities* – maintain your *productivity* – be *purposeful* in your actions – avoid *procrastination* – ignite your *passion* – *perform* like your life depends on it – *pray* often. And no matter what, maintain your *professionalism* at all times.

"Step out of the history that is holding you back. Step into the new story you are willing to create." — Oprah Winfrey, American Television Producer, Award-winning Talk Show Host, Actress, Author, and Philanthropist

#### #10. BD 101. "Out of sight, out of mind."

There has been so much uncertainty the last 18 months; our world has been turned upside down and inside out. For those of us in a sales or business development role, it has affected us severely. As soon as the pandemic hit and it occurred to everyone that it wasn't similar to the flu in that you don't just suffer and get over it within a few weeks, and that the effects could be far more devastating, a lot of people from the industry came to me for advice. Everyone wanted to know how we would continue conducting business development. A lot of seasoned business developers wondered how they would connect with their clients. What were their options? How would they continue to stay in front of them? Regardless of the circumstance or how their day-to-day activities changed, the one advice I did offer was that waiting for life to get back to normal and being dormant was not an option.

During the pandemic it's even more critical to stay present and in front of our clients; we have to be ready to offer our support when they need us. In May of 2020 after nine weeks of self-isolation and with stay-at-home orders being extended on a weekly basis, I decided to issue a survey to my top 50 key client relationships. I invited 50 decision-makers (those responsible for their capital budgets and capital improvement programs from various markets including aviation, education, health care, public agency, and transportation) and asked several business development related questions.

Within the survey, I also provided the option for them to respond freely to the last question, "What is your best advice for those of us in business development amid COVID-19 in lieu of in-person events?" One response in particular really stood out to me. The response was, "If I don't hear from you in three months or so, I am going to assume that you are no longer in business because of the pandemic." Reading that response made my heart stop. It shows that it is even more important today to ramp up our business development activities and to not dial them back because of the uncertainties.

As is the case with stereotypes, when someone or something pushes you into a corner, the last thing you should do is retreat, because going into hiding is a temporary and unproductive solution. If you are performing and doing a great job, you should be proud of your contribution and not let someone or something overshadow your efforts. Continue to be supportive of others while inserting yourself into meetings. Consistently perform. Show your value by staying present, visible, and committed to the company's goals. Let your contributions be seen and felt by your supervisors. Channel the uncertainty and negativity into real value-adding contributions.

**"Surround yourself with people that push you to do better. No drama or negativity. Just higher goals and higher motivation. Good times and positive energy. No jealousy or hate. Simply bringing out the absolute best in each other." — Warren Buffet, American Investor, Business Tycoon, Philanthropist, and Chairman and CEO of Berkshire Hathaway**

# CHAPTER 15

# WHAT MAKES YOU A GAME CHANGER? BEING FEARLESS HELPS

I am not sure how or why I became so fearless even as a young kid. For as long as I could remember my parents taught me to be brave and to be confident about who I am. They always encouraged me to ask questions, to surround myself with individuals smarter than myself, and to speak to anyone and everyone about anything. And if it happened to be a discussion I knew nothing about, they taught me to stand there and listen. Now having shared that, there are a few things that I am not comfortable being around or doing. I am not a fan of snakes, ghosts, night diving, and mathematics. Math is not my strongest suit, something you've already read about. Otherwise, there's really not much else that scares me. I am unafraid of heights, having gone skydiving before. So yes, I do enjoy jumping out of planes. Once this pandemic is under control, I plan on signing up for another skydiving experience.

In 2011, I got certified in Abu Dhabi as a diver. However, despite my love for the water and the many surprises one discovers under 60 feet of water, I have yet to do a night dive. One of my best friends in Malaysia, Oscar, swears by it. He's done so many night dives and speaks so fondly of it and the beauty/creatures he sees that he is slowly starting to convince me to try it. While it does scare me, I am intrigued by what I might see. But for the moment a night dive hasn't made its way to my bucket list.

A lot of self-help, inspirational, leadership, and business management books frequently challenge us by asking this question: What would you do if you weren't afraid? I have also asked that of myself, and my response was, "Well, I would write this book and the truth is, I am afraid. I am afraid of the criticism I might get after publishing this book. It scares me to think how people will perceive what I am sharing, my personal struggles, and my family's loss. What will people say? How will they react?"

The possibility of the negative criticisms, the naysayers, the harsh comments, and the judgements that could potentially come my way… the thought of all of that scares me. But I also know in order to make a positive difference I have to tell my story because I want other Asian and minority women to know they are not alone and what they are going through, I have gone through. The upside is, if I can learn how to survive the stereotypes and I've found a way to thrive by transforming the many yins into many yangs, then perhaps you can too.

Life is about giving and sharing, and the more you give and share of yourself, the greater the rewards.

Being fearless also means saying yes to more! And allowing yourself to be part of more adventures. Many of us spent most of 2020 reevaluating and reflecting on what's important to us, I hope that in the near future we will all aspire to be fearless.

Fearlessness is not the absence of fear. Rather, it's the mastery of fear.

To be fearless is to get up one more time after we fall or fail. The more comfortable we are about falling, the more fearless we will be, and the easier our journey will eventually become. If we look at some of these challenges more as adventures, we will allow ourselves to have more learning experiences. I have fallen many, many times and I have the physical and mental scars to prove it, but I am willing to give myself the opportunity to uncover what may be possible. When I accepted the job with Walter Sr., I was fearless. When I joined Guy Mehula at Parsons, I was fearless. When I joined him in the Middle East, I allowed myself to be fearless. And when I eventually take the night dive, that too will be an act of fearlessness.

Being an Asian immigrant in a highly male dominated industry, generally, and in the construction industry, specifically, makes me fearless. If that doesn't say it all, I don't know what will. If you haven't already noticed, I am a bit of an adventure junkie.

Being fearless doesn't mean you give up being vulnerable; it means being keenly aware of your weaknesses and learning how to disarm them. It's a delicate balance of owning who you are and realizing nothing will hold you back from your aspirations.

Here's what I love about being fearless: it gives you permission to step outside of your comfort zone and when you do that, new opportunities and relationships start to uncover themselves. Too often people feel more comfortable saying no because of fear. I want to encourage you to say "yes" more often.

Let's use my life as a case study. Clearly, I've said more yeses in my life than nos. I said yes to moving to Los Angeles when I knew no one, yes to starting out a career in an industry I knew nothing about, yes to jumping out of a plane, and most of all, yes to writing this book. I can't imagine where I would be today if not for all these yeses.

I've traveled the world because I've said yes to just about every invitation that has come my way, from international yoga retreats to vacations with my friends in countries I would have never even thought about like Nepal and Sri Lanka. I've said yes to speaking engagements with various organizations nationally and internationally and discovered how much I actually enjoy having an audience and having a dialogue during the Q&A segment with people from all over the world.

What makes me fearless is my willingness to be knocked down. The reality is that failing is a way to learn; in fact, it's probably one of the fastest ways to learn something about yourself. It also forces us to discover a new approach or strategy regarding what not to do in the future. No matter how you dissect it, as far as I am concerned being fearless is a win-win scenario.

Being fearless is as much mental as it is physical. When you are fearless, you are more mentally prepared to be knocked down, and in being prepared you are more rooted in your stance. Your physical reflects your mental being. The physical and mental are strongly connected to each other, so much so that if you are feeling confident you are automatically standing taller. Your shoulders are relaxed and pulled back, your head is lifted, and you are in your power stance. There's a lot to embrace by being fearless, because when you feel good, you tend to look better, and you are taking on each day by projecting your best self.

By being fearless, you instantly become more mentally alert and eager to contribute towards the greater good. The unity of both the physical and mental will come across as a whole. Your body language, through your posture, how you gesture and express yourself, will be reflective of the knowledge that you now carry and own in a discussion. And when you are poised in a positive way you are more likely to share an idea, and your idea will be more likely to be received because of how you deliver the message mentally and physically. At the end of the day, your body language supports your message, and being authentic while being fearless is key to delivering a successful message.

Having the power to say yes is the start of something new and as one of my mentors used to remind me, we can do whatever it is we want, as long as it's not immoral, unethical, illegal, or stupid.

Fifty percent of the population in the world is made up of women and yet we just had our first female Major League Baseball general manager and of course our first female vice president. This disparity is clearly an issue in today's society. We need more fearless women in board positions, more women in the C-suite, more women on management teams, more women calling the shots, and more women supporting other women.

Today, one in five Americans suffers from depression or some kind of mental behavior issue, and that should get everyone's attention. When we say yes to supporting each other, we are on the right path towards preventing the escalation of mental health issues. We must and can do better.

Shortly after the killing of George Floyd in Minneapolis, Minnesota, I was meeting with a client and we couldn't not discuss all the unrest that was happening in the country. Dr. Rueben Smith, Chief Facilities Executive of the Los Angeles Community College

District (LACCD), the largest community college district in the country, reminds us that it is not enough to not be racist, we have to be anti-racist. And to be anti-racist is to be fearless.

Racism is not a feeling or emotion, it is a way of thinking, creating, and implementing policies that provide preferences and privileges to a certain race. As a community we must work together to do away with such inequalities. Much like stereotypes, racism is not a trait we are born with. It is a learned behavior and over time, it's what societies have shaped us to believe.

In addition, when you are fearless, you allow yourself to discover a fresh perspective either about yourself or someone else. It clears the path for a new direction, random friendships, and sometimes a passion you've been wanting to look into. To be fearless doesn't mean you have to start with something big, it can involve starting something small, having a conversation about something uncomfortable, or asking for help. But whatever direction you choose to start with, never underestimate the power of doing something, especially if you're doing the right thing.

My parents had high expectations of me. I was always expected to do the right thing and that in hindsight prepared me for a complex, judgmental, and challenging world. They never sugar-coated how hard life was going to be; sometimes they didn't even have to express that in words, I witnessed it in their struggles and their compassion for others.

They had equipped me with the fundamentals. Our core values were to always be respectful, be kind to each other, and to share (whenever possible) a laugh, a meal, a moment in time. Show genuine gratitude when others are kind to you and operate with integrity because your reputation is ultimately your legacy.

Of course, my sister and I are constantly reminded that we are products of our parents; we are representatives of the "Lee" last name and must carry it with distinct honor and humility. Everything we do is a reflection of how our parents raised us. So, thank you, Mom and Dad, for your guidance, your patience, your unconditional love, and the courage to be fearless.

Here's someone who decided to be fearless....

**"I never wanted to be the next Bruce Lee. I just wanted to be the first Jackie Chan." — Jackie Chan**

# Chapter 16

# Fear of Missing Out (FOMO)

I've never been one of those individuals who had the fear of missing out syndrome. Oddly enough I was never a trend follower. I cherished things that lasted a lifetime; I appreciated longevity. Even as a child I was never one to only look for trendy items and I certainly didn't care about being a trendsetter. What I did worry about was not winning a swim meet or disappointing my tennis team. As an adult, I worried about not being sufficiently prepared for a meeting or a discussion. I hated that feeling. I would feel so inadequate and that would drive me crazy. After all, I'm an Asian woman and I'm supposed to be one of the smartest people in the room, right?

Over the years I've been able to channel this fear by over-preparing for all of my meetings, really coming in with an understanding of the 5 W's – the who, what, why, when, and where. I believe that for any meeting, if you can come in having some basic knowledge of each pursuit and some basic understanding of the opportunity, you are already more knowledgeable than most people in the room.

Unfortunately, fear is a very real thing and I want to encourage all of you to use your fear in a positive way. Because I disliked being unprepared for any discussion, I would often over-prepare and that has always worked in my favor. I've never heard of someone failing on an assignment by being overly prepared, have you?

The fear of missing out however, implies you are somehow in-adequate compared to your friends, especially if you are not in the loop of the latest trends, styles, technologies, or social media posts. FOMO is characterized by the desire to stay continually connected with what others are doing and is particularly evident in how mil-lennials function today. In today's social media-driven world, FOMO encourages an overload of sharing, driven by attention and an unpar-alleled engagement of all senses 24 hours a day, seven days a week.

Based on how this theory works, I'd like to see the concept of FOMO applied in a more productive and meaningful way. As an example, when women accomplish great things and overcome un-breakable barriers, I'd like to see us rally behind their accomplish-ments. I'd like to hear about it, and I'd like the opportunity to cele-brate with them. I don't want their sacrifices and accomplishments to go unnoticed. These advancements and reasons for jubilation are what I fear missing out on. We live and move in such a fast-paced world that sometimes we don't take the time to pause, to celebrate, and to honor each other's triumphs. These are moments I'd like to experience and cherish and not miss out on.

I also don't want the men in our lives to be left out of the pro-cess of change. I want to welcome and encourage them to join us as women make advancements in equity, diversity, and inclusivity. This is not a man-versus-woman scenario. This is all of us coming together so we can support one another.

I fear that as women continue to make strides and make our voices heard, men will begin to feel left out. That is something I want to avoid at all cost.

I want to encourage all the men to join us, as women continue to push the status quo and accomplish great things. I want to ensure that the other half of the population is right there celebrating along with us. I also want to applaud and recognize all the men who have stepped up in support of women. The greatest, most positive influences in my life have all been men and I am grateful for that.

At the same time, I am also acutely aware that some men continue to be intimidated by independent and successful women. The truth is, despite our success and independence we want and need the support from men. Since I work in a male dominated industry, I have had men approach me with this question: How can men take a more active role in support of women? How can we help you be more successful?

Here is how I have responded:

1. Invite them to take a seat at the table.
2. Give them a voice, an opportunity to express their opinion.
3. Support their ideas.
4. Offer to help execute the ideas.
5. Speak highly of their contributions to the team.
6. Share the credit; give credit when it is due.
7. Be a mentor and coach; help develop their potential.
8. Don't allow them to fail.
9. Expand their roles; give them a larger platform/promotion.
10. Try not to be intimidated by them.

In summary, I want to encourage you to leverage these stereo-types to your advantage by transforming them into opportunities for positive change:

1.  Use these opportunities to motivate and fuel your perfor-mance. Your performance will speak volumes about who you are, your ability to stay focused on the overall objectives, and most of all, your capacity to positively contribute to your team.

2.  When you encounter someone who undermines your value and belittles you in front of others, immediately pivot to doing something positive for someone else. Channel that surge of energy into doing something good, whether it's for someone else in the office, a friend, or a charity. Use that energy to give back to someone who needs your positivity.

3.  When someone puts you down, discredits your knowledge, or embarrasses you in front of a colleague, immediately plan on doing something good for yourself, right after work. Going for a run, showing up at the gym, attending a yoga class, booking a tee time to golf on the weekend with your friends, having Happy Hour with a friend outside of work are all activities to help you deal with the stresses at work. These activities will help you look forward to something pos-itive while doing something healthy for yourself. It will also allow you to release the negative energy and will reenergize you about what's truly important. For me, those activities are a great way to devise how I am going to come back even better and stronger to exceed expectations.

4.  When you are snubbed by someone, choose to be kinder to them. I know it's not easy, but give them the benefit of the doubt. I always assume when someone else is behaving in a

really unbecoming way, they are having a bad day and they are just taking it out on the people around them. Do you remember the saying I referenced earlier, "Kill them with kindness"? Well, it really does work. I always cut people some slack for their rudeness, disrespect, and unwarranted comments. When we are kind, we choose to be responsible for our actions. And really, all we can control is how we react to different people and situations.

5. Share the credit, no matter what. Even if the individual giving you the most grief didn't do his or her part and is always taking credit for everything, share the credit anyway. It's the right and professional thing to do and will add to your credibility as a leader and team player. At the end of the day, you would know that you took the high road by acknowledging everyone on the team. A true leader always shares the credit with the team. And believe me, someone always notices; people always know the truth as to who was behind all the strategy, relationship building, and hard work.

6. Find a strong advocate personally and professionally, internally and externally. Someone who has a voice stronger than yours and who has influence. Someone who can back you up regarding your work ethic, integrity, and ability to deliver. Someone who will sing your praises. An advocate who will back you up when you are not in the room, an advocate who will speak up on your behalf based on integrity, trust, and honesty.

7. Find an organization or a group that values your opinion, one that you can be a part of where your skill sets and contributions are needed, so you can feel good about yourself while contributing in a positive and meaningful way. This will in

turn improve your self-esteem and will support a deeper connection with others.

8. Collaborate to combat negativity, go out of your way to support different groups within the company. It's great for character building and it leaves a positive, lasting impression everywhere you go.

9. Be the gold standard of teamwork, be highly collaborative, communicate often and skillfully, always operate with humility, integrity, and kindness.

10. Make every day a great day! Wake up grateful, smiling, and ready to take on the world. If you are currently in a very stressful and contentious work environment, find a support group – a team of friends who are there to listen to you and who can help guide you. This is where having a great mentor can be extremely beneficial. If you have exercised all options to be productive and happy at work and continue to be miserable, it may be time to look at other options.

Ultimately, focus on you and your development.

### "Be so good, they can't ignore you." — Steve Martin, American Actor and Comedian

Make your performance your brand and reputation and know that while history may shape who you are, your future is whatever you make of it.

I want to encourage you to make the most of all the yins and the yangs that come your way. I am so blessed to have the best of both worlds – my Asian culture and traditions and my American life with an abundance of possibilities. I've been able to extract the best from each to create my unique story.

With the right mindset and under the right conditions, the convergence of multiple events, the blending of ideas, supportive team members, and encouraging parents, or with any combination of these factors, I am confident the future will continue to be promising and filled with hope not just for me, but for all of us. Embrace all of who you are, your slightly slanted eyes, your tan skin tone, your curly hair and freckles, your inner strength, and your ability to rise to any occasion. Be relentlessly passionate about all things good, kind, and compassionate, and together we can make a difference.

You owe it to yourself to live your best life. Don't let the sacrifices of your parents and all those who fought so hard for you and for us to go to waste. We've made a lot of strides as women and as minorities but there's clearly more progress to be made.

If you found comfort in this book and found it to be relatable to parts of your life and feel it can support and be an inspiration to someone else, please feel free to share my stories. I invite you to ask yourself, what will your call to action be today, now, and from here on out? You can start by doing something small, by sharing this book with your sisters, friends, and maybe even a perfect stranger. But do something good and genuine.

Don't live in fear and in hesitation. In many ways, this is your time and your year to unmask yourself. The power in sharing our experiences and struggles is a form of survival and sustainment for all of us. If you can, make a difference in a substantive way; pay it forward. Help recruit the best and most diverse talent. Let's retain, reimagine, and re-energize our efforts so we can all construct a future that welcomes and represents all women.

With the right mindset and approach, you too can leverage stereotypes to your advantage. Remember, the best is yet to come and it's waiting for you.

"The secret to an extraordinary life is to demand more from yourself than anyone else could possibly expect – raise your standards."
— Tony Robbins, *New York Times* Best-selling Author, Life and Business Strategist, Philanthropist, and Entrepreneur

# Call to Action

**Do your part, challenge yourself. Pledge your support in advancement of all women.**

I am calling on all men and women, but especially women around the world, to make a conscientious effort to support other women regardless of the industry you represent and the position you hold, irrespective of cultural backgrounds, gender, and ethnicity. Whether you choose to be someone's big sister, mentor, or role model, I challenge women today to identify one or two individuals they can support personally and professionally. Together we can make a difference.

**To sign this pledge and to join the movement, please go to my website, www.diannelee88.com.**

When you sign this pledge, you have made a personal commitment to yourself to lead by example:

By judging less and praising more

By being a life-long student so you can continue to share your knowledge

By staying authentic and genuine so others can appreciate your true value

By developing specific measures to address the elevation and visibility of women

By remembering all those who have paved the way for us to have a voice and a vote

By celebrating each other's successes and inspiring others in their personal journeys

By acknowledging that we all have a different story and therefore bring a different perspective

By creating a welcoming and inclusive environment where gender equality is a core value

By supporting, encouraging, empowering, and advocating for meaningful engagement in leadership roles

By accepting each other, taking the time to understand one's culture and background and what makes her unique